☐ NATIONAL GEOGRAPHIC
Reach
for Reading™

COMMON CORE PROGRAM

☐ NATIONAL GEOGRAPHIC LEARNING

 CENGAGE Learning®

Acknowledgments

Grateful acknowledgment is given to the authors, artists, photographers, museums, publishers, and agents for permission to reprint copyrighted material. Every effort has been made to secure the appropriate permission. If any omissions have been made or if corrections are required, please contact the Publisher.

Cover illustration: Joel Sotelo

Cover Design and Art Direction: Visual Asylum

Illustration Credits: All PM illustrations by National Geographic Learning.

For product information and technology assistance, contact us at
Customer & Sales Support, 888-915-3276

For permission to use material from this text or product, submit all requests online at **www.cengage.com/permissions**
Further permissions questions can be emailed to
permissionrequest@cengage.com

National Geographic Learning | Cengage Learning
1 Lower Ragsdale Drive
Building 1, Suite 200
Monterey, CA 93940

Cengage Learning is a leading provider of customized learning solutions with office locations around the globe, including Singapore, the United Kingdom, Australia, Mexico, Brazil, and Japan. Locate your local office at **www.cengage.com/global**.

Cengage Learning products are represented in Canada by Nelson Education, Ltd.

Visit National Geographic Learning online at **NGL.Cengage.com**
Visit our corporate website a **www.cengage.com**

Printed in the USA.
Quad/Graphics, Versailles, KY,

ISBN: 978-13054-99027 (Practice Book)

ISBN: 978-13056-58721 (Practice Masters)

Teachers are authorized to reproduce the practice masters in this book in limited quantity and solely for use in their own classrooms.

Printed in the United States of America
21 22 23 24
16 15 14

Contents

Unit 5: Everything Changes

Unit 6: Better Together

Unit 7: Best Buddies

Unit 8: Our United States

Phonics

Words with *i, ie, igh*

Circle the word that names the picture.

1.	2.	3.
(tie)	lime	chillled
tea	late	child
tail	light	chipped

4.	5.	6.
sigh	peas	three
say	pays	thigh
sea	pies	throw

7.	8.	9.
night	fate	crows
neat	fight	cries
nine	feet	cribs

10.	11.	12.
kit	flies	leaking
kite	flights	liking
kind	flows	lightning

Read It Together   The child flies the kite up high.

PM5.1

Unit 5 | Everything Changes

Name _____ Date _____

My Favorite Story

Make a theme chart to tell the details about a favorite story.

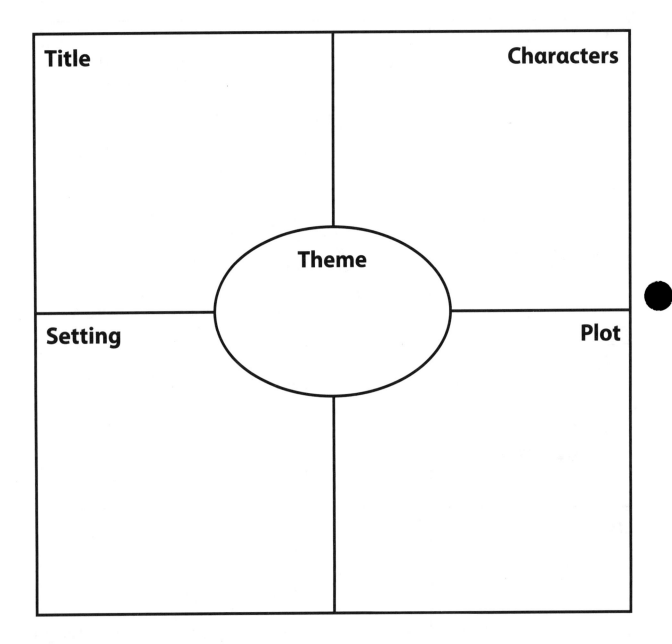

Title

Characters

Theme

Setting

Plot

 Work with a partner to find the theme of your story.

Name _____ Date _____

Words with *i, ie, igh*

Write the words to complete each sentence.

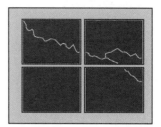

1. nightlight   child

The _____ turns on the _____.

2. lies   sighs

He _____ down in bed and _____.

3. right   silent

He likes it when the house is as _____ as it is

_____ now!

4. lights   night

All of a sudden, something _____ up the _____.

5. upright   lightning

Some _____ strikes, and he sits _____.

6. bright   fright

It is quite _____, and he is filled with _____.

7. cries   find

He _____ out and runs to _____ his mom.

8. delight   pie

They eat some _____, and he is filled with _____!

● Word Cards: Words with *i, ie, igh*

pie	lightning	child	night
flies	find	mild	thigh
nightlight	slight	skies	untied
lies	fright	mind	silent
bright	highway	fight	tie
sigh	vie	iris	necktie
pilot	kind	die	wild

● High Frequency Word Cards

don't	morning
door	air
about	earth
work	hear
should	near
want	even
where	round
important	start
sound	here

Name _____ Date _____

Words with *kn, gn, wr, mb*

Circle the word that names the picture.

1. sun (sign) seen	**2.** climb click cling	**3.** wring wife knife
4. white write knight	**5.** roam gnome comb	**6.** kit knit quit
7. wrench bench drench	**8.** long lamb last	**9.** three know knee
10. gnat wrap knot	**11.** gnash kneel wreath	**12.** thud thumb think

Read It Together Show me your thumb, your wrist, and your knee.

Name _____ Date _____

Round and Round

Write a word from the box to complete each sentence.

High Frequency **Words**
air
earth
even
hear
here
morning
near
round
sound
start

1. They _____ the ride, and I go round and round.

2. I _____ the sound of the music playing.

3. I see the _____ spinning by.

4. I feel the warm morning _____ blowing on me.

5. Now we are getting _____ the end of the ride.

6. The ride was _____ more fun this time than it was before!

7. I think I will come back _____ to go on this ride one more time.

Name _____ Date _____

Use Question Words

Grammar Rules Question Words

Questions that ask for more information often start with
Who, What, Where, Why, When, or *How.*

Who asks about a person.	*Why* asks for a reason.
What asks about a thing.	*When* asks about a time.
Where asks about a place.	*How* asks how things happen.

Each sentence needs a question word. Spell the question word that belongs with each sentence by filling in the blanks. Work with a partner to see who can complete the word first.

1. __ h __ tells you about weather in your city?

2. W __ __ did it snow early this year?

3. __ __ w does a thermometer work?

4. __ __ e __ will spring begin?

5. W __ __ __ happens when ice melts?

6. __ h __ __ __ is the hottest place on Earth?

Name _____ Date _____

Words with *kn, gn, wr, mb*

Write the words to complete each sentence.

1. crumbs   wrens

The _____ might like _____ to eat.

2. wrap   know

I _____ how to _____ them in a napkin.

3. knapsack   knot

Just tie a _____. Then put them in my _____.

4. climb   lambs

We will _____ up this hill and pass those _____.

5. kneel   limb

Then we can _____ under a _____ of this tree.

6. wrists   gnats

Oh, no! The _____ are starting to bite my _____.

7. knack   wrecking

They have a _____ for _____ the day!

8. wrens   crumbs

We'll leave the _____ for the _____ to eat and go back home.

Name _____   Date _____

Write Sentences

Read the letter. Then choose an end mark from the box that goes with each sentence. You may use each end mark as many times as you want.

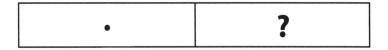

Hi Grandma,

Thank you very much for the fleece jacket __•__ Can

you guess where I am going to wear it ____ Our class is

going to the farm next Saturday ____ It might be cold,

so I will wear my new fleece jacket ____ Who told you

blue was my favorite color ____ I bet it was Dad ____

Love,

Marcie

Name _____   Date _____

When the Wind Stops

Use clues from the story to figure out the theme.

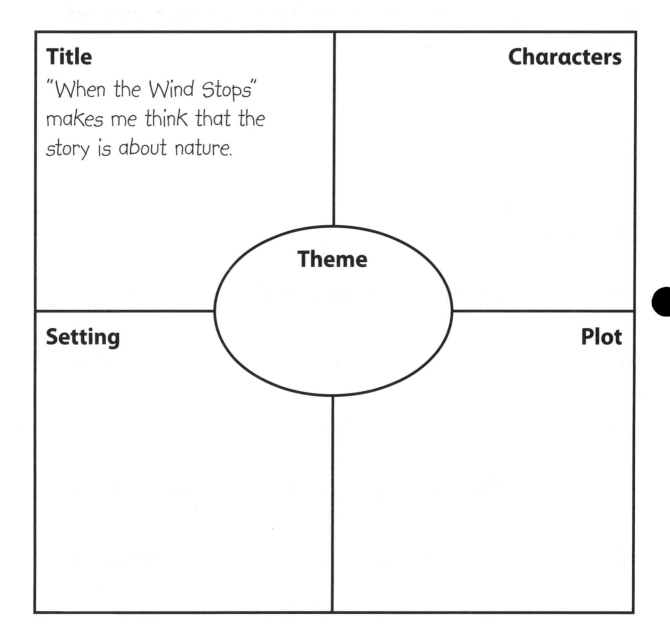

Title
"When the Wind Stops" makes me think that the story is about nature.

Characters

Theme

Setting

Plot

💬 **Share your clues and theme with a partner.**

Name _____ Date _____

Words with -y

Circle the word that names the picture.

1. cry / crayon / crusty	**2.** hockey / happy / hilly	**3.** know / keep / key
4. maybe / my / money	**5.** bunny / baby / by	**6.** flow / fly / fluffy
7. chimney / chilly / chatty	**8.** myself / mighty / muddy	**9.** pokey / pony / pry
10. skinny / sigh / sky	**11.** donkey / dry / dolly	**12.** 50 filthy / fry / fifty

Read It Together Will you try to ride a pony or a donkey?

Name _____ Date _____

Words with -y

Write the words to complete each sentence.

1. puppy   Billy

_____ puts a leash on his _____.

2. slowly   hilly

Then they hike _____ up a _____ path.

3. chilly   sky

It is _____ on top, but the _____ is blue and sunny.

4. valley   tiny

The people look _____ in the _____ below them.

5. smoky   chimneys

Billy sees _____ air coming out of the _____.

6. quickly   windy

All of a sudden, it gets very _____, so Billy and his pup

run back _____.

7. gusty   by

A leaf blows _____ them in the _____ wind. Then
another leaf, and another!

8. cozy   happy

Billy is _____ to get back to his _____ home!

Phonics

Plurals -s, -es, ies

tail	+ s	= tails
dish	+ es	= dishes
bunny	– y + ies	= bunnies

Write the word with the correct ending to complete each sentence.

1. dog

   I have two _____.

2. baby

   One of them had six _____ last month.

3. puppy

   All of the _____ are black and white.

4. patch

   One is black with white _____ on his body.

5. nose

   Two are all white with black _____.

6. tummy

   Three are black with white _____.

7. box

   All the pups sleep in _____ with blankets inside.

8. family

   I will miss them when their _____ pick them up
   next month.

● Word Cards: Words with -y

jelly	skyline	penny	fly
study	trying	slowly	why
daily	myself	many	why
imaginary	sky	python	fry
heavy	by	sly	very
fancy	January	worry	deny
quickly	dry	carry	type

● High Frequency Word Cards

house	blue
kind	fall
place	also
both	first
been	most
great	family
friend	mountain
different	only
many	every

Name _____ Date _____

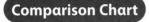

Compare Author's Purpose

**Show why Charlotte Zolotow wrote "When the Wind Stops."
Compare this to why Glen Phelan wrote "Day and Night."**

Charlotte Zolotow	Glen Phelan
• to tell about how nature changes	• to tell about changes in nature

 Tell a partner which selection you liked better. Explain your favorite author's purpose for writing.

Phonics

Words with Soft *c* and *g*

Sort the words by hard and soft sounds.

cell	gel	candy	gold
cuts	price	badge	spaceship
gallop	changing	flag	picnic

city

1. _____

2. _____

3. _____

cap

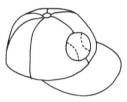

4. _____

5. _____

6. _____

gem

7. _____

8. _____

9. _____

gate

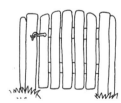

10. _____

11. _____

12. _____

Name _____ Date _____

How to Get There

Write a word from the box to complete each sentence.

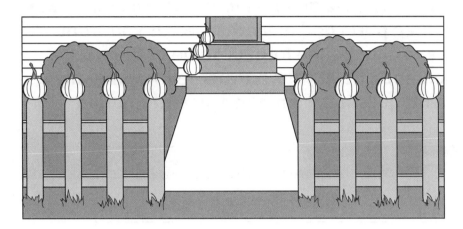

High Frequency Words
also
blue
every
fall
family
first
many
most
mountain
only

Dear Debby,

Here's how to get to my house. First,

go past the road to the _____. You will see a bright

pink house with a _____ door. It _____ has bright

green trim. You can't miss it. There is _____ one

house like it! Then go to the right. You will see my house.

It's the one with _____ pumpkins on the fence. My

_____ puts them there every fall. This fall, we have

the _____ pumpkins ever! I can't wait to see you!

Your pal,

Henry

Name _____   Date _____

Mix and Match Sentences

First choose a naming part from column A. Then choose a telling part from column B. Then choose an end mark from column C. Say a sentence using all three parts and any other words you want to add. You may have to change the form of some of the words. After you say your sentence, have your partner tell whether the sentence is a statement, question, command, or exclamation.

A	B	C
I	like	.
Jake	blow	?
Mom	fall	!
our principal	talk	
you	is / are	
the sun	sound	
the rain	feel	
the wind	was / were	
leaves	go	
trees	begin	
it	end	
they	fall	

Phonics

Words with Soft *c* and *g*

Write the word that completes each sentence.

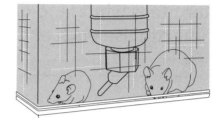

1. city   fringe   cotton

Cindy lives in the _____.

2. hug   huge   hedge

She can have pets, but they can't be _____.

3. gems   cells   mice

That's why Cindy has two pet _____.

4. nice   cage   badge

Her pets live in a screen _____.

5. space   page   cent

The mice have lots of _____ to hide and to play.

6. lace   judge   climb

The pets like to _____ up the side of the cage.

7. smudge   judge   race

They like to _____ around on their wheel.

8. fancies   changes   genies

Sometimes Cindy _____ the food she gives her pets.

9. rice   range   bridge

They can eat _____ and oats or food from the pet shop.

Grammar and Writing

Write Four Kinds of Sentences

Read the story. Then choose the end mark and letter from the box that tells what kind of sentence each is and write them on the line. You can use each end mark and letter as many times as you want.

.	?	!	
S (Statement)	**Q** (Questions)	**C** (Command)	**E** (Exclamation)

That is the most beautiful tree in the whole world

<u>! E</u> It's right here in our schoolyard ____ Do you know

why the leaves change colors ____ I learned about it

in school ____ Sit down, and I will tell you what I know

____ Stop talking, and listen to me ____

Name _____   Date _____

Build Sentences

1. Play with a partner.

2. Use the words below to build sentences. Write a question, a statement, a command, and an exclamation.

3. Begin with a capital letter. Add an end mark.

4. The player who first writes all four types of sentences correctly wins.

Is / is	night	beautiful
The / the	Do / do	star
Your / your	see	shadow
Come / come	get	you
Are / are	book	That / that

_____

_____

_____

_____

_____

Phonics

Words with *oo*, *ue*

Circle the word that names the picture.

1. zigzag / zee / (zoo)	**2.** spoon / spin / Spain	**3.** glow / glee / glue
4. bloom / blow / blue	**5.** rays / roots / rows	**6.** shoot / shot / shut
7. bait / bat / boot	**8.** try / true / tray	**9.** reef / roof / rude
10. hoop / hop / hope	**11.** main / moon / moan	**12.** die / due / day

Read It Together   Is it true that a shoot has roots and buds?

Name _____ Date _____

Compare and Contrast

Complete the comparison chart below.

Picture Cards	How They Are Alike	How They Are Different
Picture Card 1: _____		
Picture Card 2: _____		

 Share your chart with a partner. Tell how your picture cards are alike and different.

Name _____ Date _____

Words with *oo, ue*

Write the word that completes each sentence.

1. clueless proof moonlight

I wake up and see an animal in the _____.

2. due raccoon room

It is a big _____ with a black mask!

3. snooping true bamboo

I think it is _____ around my trash cans to find food.

4. clues fools moods

What are my _____?

5. roof Tuesday boom

I hear a clang and then a _____!

6. bedroom dues clueless

At first I am _____ about what to do.

7. spoon glued bloom

Then I open the window and bang a pan with
a _____.

8. igloo scoot blue

While I bang, I yell so that animal will _____.

9. zooms fondues shampoos

It _____ away into the trees. Now I can snooze!

● Word Cards: Words with *oo, ue*

raccoon	glue	pool	root
balloon	bedroom	avenue	zoom
blue	zoo	igloo	accrue
tooth	moonlight	swoon	duel
fool	proof	true	room
untrue	shampoo	clues	scoot
due	gruel	pursue	unglue

● High Frequency Word Cards

may	full
ever	above
nice	far
thank	something
push	goes
around	better
teacher	long
would	talk
while	watch

Name _____ Date _____

Phonics

Endings *-er, -est*

Cut out the cards and mix them up. Sort them by ending. Explain the spelling changes.

fast	**close**
faster	**closer**
fastest	**closest**
sad	**happy**
sadder	**happier**
saddest	**happiest**

Name _____ Date _____

What Is It?

Write a word from the box to complete each sentence.

High Frequency Words
above
better
far
full
goes
long
something
talk
watch
while

1. What do I like to _____ ? I'll give you some clues.

2. It is something far _____ me up in the sky.

3. I like to _____ about its phases.

4. When it is full, it shines brightly _____ I sleep.

5. Two weeks later, the light _____ away, and I can't see it!

6. It is not out of sight for a _____ time.

7. That's good, because I like it _____ when I can see it! What is it?

Name _____ Date _____

Use Yes/No Questions

Directions:

1. Make a spinner.

2. Play with a partner.

3. Take turns spinning the spinner.

4. Read the sentence frame. Ask a question using **is**, **are**, **does**, or **do**. Then have your partner answer the question with a yes/no answer.

Make a Spinner
1. Put a paper clip over the center of the spinner.
2. Touch the point of a pencil on the middle of the wheel and through the loop of the paper clip.
3. Spin the paper clip to make a spinner.

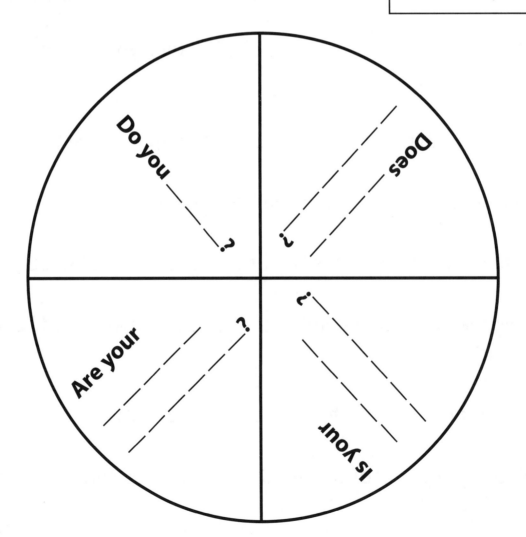

Phonics

Endings -*er*, -*est*

Write the word with the correct ending to complete each sentence.

cold			+ er	= colder
brave	– e		+ er	= braver
sad		+d	+ er	= sadder
lucky	– y	+ i	+ er	= luckier
cold			+ est	= coldest
brave	– e		+ est	= bravest
sad	+d		+ est	= saddest
lucky	– y	+ i	+ est	= luckiest

1. close

I live _____ to the beach than Hal.

2. sunny

We pick the _____ days of all to go.

3. hot

Those days can be the _____ days of all, too.

4. tasty

My dad gives us peaches because they are _____ than plums. That's what I think!

5. fast

We have a race to see if Hal swims _____ than I swim.

6. big

Then we jump into the _____ waves.

7. nice

I have a _____ time at the beach with Hal than by myself.

8. happy

We're the _____ of all the kids at the beach!

Write Compound Sentences

Read the story. Then choose a word from the box that goes with each sentence. You can use each word as many times as you want.

and	but

My family is going for a walk in the park. I am

wearing my light jacket, ___*but*___ my little brother is

wearing his heavy coat. The sun is shining brightly,

_____ the wind is chilly. It is early spring, _____

there are some flowers starting to bloom. Winter

is gone, _____ we will still have some cold days.

Some girls are playing soccer, _____ some boys are

watching them. My big sister loves spring, _____

so do I.

Name _____ Date _____

What Makes the Seasons?

Complete the comparison chart below. Show how the seasons are alike and different.

	Spring	Summer	Fall	Winter
Leaves	sprout			
Raindrops	fall			
Snow	melts			
Days	get longer			

 Use the information from the chart to tell your partner how the seasons are alike and different.

Phonics

Words with *ue, ew, ui, ou*

Read the sentences and sort the underlined words by sound.

1. <u>Sue</u> sits in the shade under a tree.

2. She is eating <u>fruit</u> when she hears sounds above her.

3. She looks up and sees a <u>few</u> cats stuck in a tree.

4. The cats <u>mew</u> and mew.

5. A <u>group</u> of people comes to help the cats.

6. The crew <u>rescues</u> the cats from the tree.

1. _____   **4.** _____

2. _____   **5.** _____

3. _____   **6.** _____

Name _____ Date _____

Words with *ue, ew, ui, ou*

Write the words to complete each sentence.

1. choose   foods

What _____ do you _____ to eat?

2. blew   soup

Tam has hot _____ for lunch, but she just _____ on it to make it cooler.

3. stew   chews

Manny _____ the chunks of meat in his

yummy _____.

4. fruit   juice

Kim likes _____ from different kinds of _____.

5. Sue   Tuesday

Every _____, my friend _____ eats hot dogs and beans.

6. few   cashews

Loc mixes raisins with a _____ kinds of nuts, like

_____ and peanuts.

7. fondue   new

My family wants to try something _____, so we're

making _____.

● Words with *ew, ui, ou, ue*

jewel	fruit	cruise	soup
cue	fewer	rescue	you
crew	continue	virtue	wound
● bruised	hue	nephew	chew
argue	pewter	grew	group
new	rouge	screw-driver	blew
● juice	knew	value	statue

For use with TE p. T319g   **PM5.37**   Unit 5 | Everything Changes

High Frequency Word Cards

yes	again
say	between
write	almost
dear	never
name	went
letter	any
says	below
answer	grow
tomorrow	surprise

For use with TE p. T319g   **PM5.38**   **Unit 5** | Everything Changes

Name _____ Date _____

Venn Diagram

Compare Genres

Use the Venn diagram to tell how "What Makes the Seasons?" and "A Winter Wonder" are alike and different.

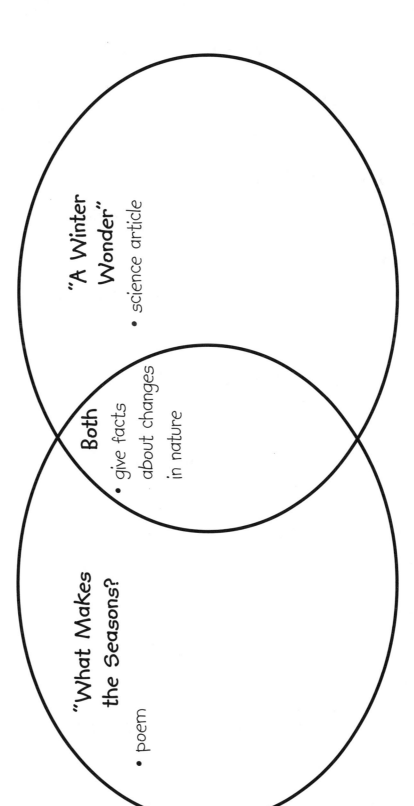

"A Winter Wonder"
• science article

Both
• give facts about changes in nature

"What Makes the Seasons?"
• poem

Tell a partner one way the selections are the same and one way they are different.

Phonics

Endings -s, -es, -ed, -ing

Write the word that completes each sentence.

1. likes   planning

Ralph _____ animals.

2. chewed   studies

He _____ them when he is outside.

3. hiked   flies

Last week, Ralph _____ near the mountains.

4. spotted   growing

He _____ some deer and a moose.

5. smiling   tried

He _____ to take some photos, but the animals ran away.

6. fixed   jogging

Now Ralph is _____ at the beach.

7. hopping   hoping

He is _____ to see some seagulls.

8. bloomed   catches

He does see one! It swoops down and _____ a fish!

9. carrying   snooped

Now it is _____ its food away.

Name _____ Date _____

Surprises

Write a word from the box to complete each sentence.

High Frequency **Words**
again
almost
any
below
between
grow
never
surprise
tomorrow
went

Mom had a _____ for me last

weekend. I went to my swim class and

came back _____ 2:00 and 2:30. I never expected

to see _____ friends at my house. That's why I

_____ jumped a mile high when all my friends yelled,

"Surprise!" We hit a homemade donkey once, and then

we hit it _____. It broke, and treats fell onto the grass

_____. Now I have a surprise for Mom. Tomorrow we

will plant a tree. Then we will watch it _____.

Grammar: Questions

Match Sentences

First read a statement in column A. Then find the question in column B that is made from that statement. Draw a line from the statement to the question. Take turns with a partner.

A	B
That is your hat.	Is it raining outside?
I am in the second grade.	Is she my aunt?
We are best friends.	Are they big and strong?
It is raining outside.	Is he late for school?
She is my aunt.	Am I on your team?
I am a soccer player.	Are we best friends?
They are big and strong.	Is that your hat?
I am on your team.	Are you funny?
He is late for school.	Am I in the second grade?
You are funny.	Am I a soccer player?

Phonics

Endings -s, -es, -ed, -ing

Write the word with the correct ending that completes each sentence.

hum	+ s	= hums	like + s = likes	cry – y + i + es	= cries
hum + m + ed	= hummed	like – e + ed = liked	cry – y + i + ed	= cried
hum + m + ing	= humming	like – e + ing = liking	cry + ing	= crying

1. bake

Last week, Dad and I _____ a pecan pie.

2. plan

We were _____ to bring it to Grandma.

3. try

The pie smelled so good that we _____ a bite.

4. taste

Soon my mom was _____ it, too.

5. stop

By the time we _____ eating, there was no pie left!

6. make

Now we are _____ Grandma a cake.

7. dry

I wash dishes and Dad _____ them, while the cake bakes.

8. write

Mom _____ a sign for the cake. It says, "No eating!"

Grammar and Writing

Write Questions

Read the letter. Then choose a word from the box that goes with each sentence.

Who	What	When	Where	Why	How

Dear Richard,

_____How_____ are you and your family? Everyone here is fine. I have a lot of questions about your trip to Mexico. _____ did you get back from your trip? Was the weather nice? _____ did you stay? Did you stay in a hotel or in a condo? _____ was your favorite activity? I bet it was snorkeling. You wrote me a postcard from Mexico. _____ did you choose a postcard with a palm tree on it? You made me want to go on a trip, too! _____ took care of your dog and birds while you were gone? Write back as soon as you can.

Your friend,

Ramesh

Use Punctuation

Grammar Rules Questions

- A question ends with a question mark. (?)
- The answer to a question ends with a period. (.)

Add correct punctuation to each of the sentences.

1. Who likes winter as much as I do

2. Many people think winter is a great season

3. Is it because there are fun things to do in the snow

4. Yes, I think it is

5. What are your favorite winter activities

6. I like to sled, ski, and build forts in the snow

7. Do you ever get cold in winter

8. No, I do not get cold because I dress warmly

Phonics

Words with *ar*

Use paper fasteners and paper clips to make two spinners. Spin them both and use the letters to make words below. If the letters don't make a word, spin again.

Make Spinners
1. Push a brad through the center of the spinner.
2. Open the brad on the back.
3. Hook a paper clip over the brad on the front to make a spinner.

Beginning of word

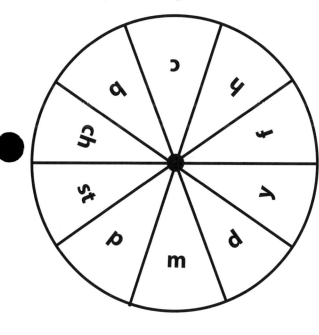

End of word

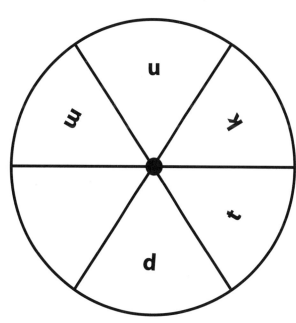

1. ___c a r___

2. ___a r___

3. ___a r___

4. ___a r___

5. ___b a r k___

6. ___a r___

7. ___a r___

8. ___a r___

9. ___a r___

10. ___a r___

11. ___a r___

12. ___a r___

Name _____ Date _____

Story Elements

Use a story map to tell about the characters, setting, and plot of a story.

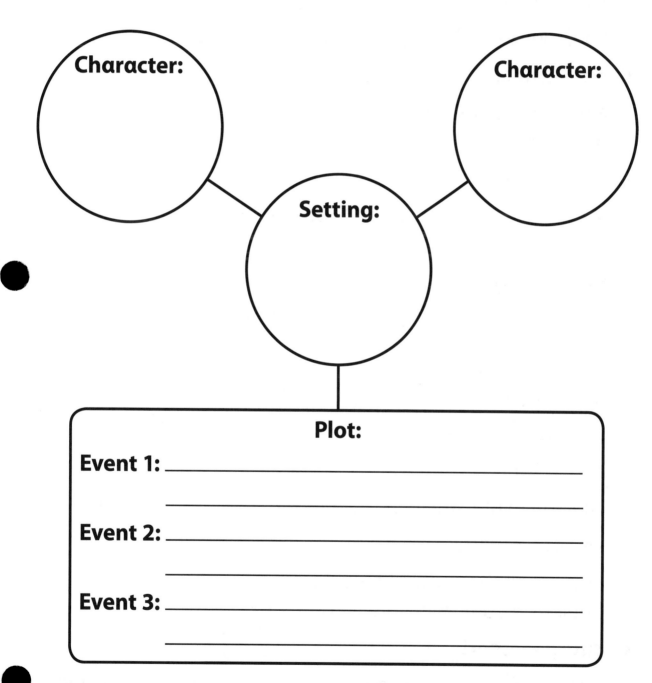

Character:

Character:

Setting:

Plot:

Event 1: _____

_____

Event 2: _____

_____

Event 3: _____

_____

 Use your story map to tell a partner a story about being part of a team.

For use with TE p. T335a   **PM6.2**   Unit 6 | Better Together

Name _____ Date _____

Words with *ar*

Write the words to complete each sentence.

1. yard   shark

Look outside. Would you see a _____ in the _____?

2. car   parked

No! You might see a _____ that is _____ in the driveway!

3. Mars   farm

Visit a local _____. Would you see the planet _____ there?

4. barn   large

No! You might see _____ bales of hay inside the _____.

5. dark   start

Look up at the _____ sky at midnight. Would you see the sun _____ to shine?

6. far   stars

No! You might see _____ that are very _____ away.

7. smart   march

Look at all the snow. Would it be _____ to _____ outside in your swimsuit?

8. charge   scarf

No! You might put on your jacket, _____, hat, boots, and mittens and then _____ outside to play in the snow!

● Word Cards: Words with *ar*

charm	farm	car	jar
charge	dart	march	far
harp	bar	jar	fort
mar	par	hate	tar
chart	purrs	art	card
for	part	tart	tarp
tore	hard	lard	north

For use with TE p. T331k   **PM6.4**   Unit 6 | Better Together

High Frequency Word Cards

here	get
near	buy
morning	old
air	just
earth	school
hear	children
sound	found
start	began
round	another
even	together

Name _____ Date _____

Longer Words with *ar*

Circle the word that names the picture.

1.
garnish
gumdrop
(garden)

2.
artist
army
attic

3.
mattress
market
marshland

4.
stoplight
starfish
sandwich

5.
magnet
margin
mammal

6.
yippee
yellow
yardstick

7.
catnap
carpet
carton

8.
partner
party
parking

9.
cartoon
classroom
charcoal

10.
garlic
gateway
gallop

11.
parsley
partway
postmark

Mary Smith
1050 Oak Street
Monterey, California
93940

12.
boxcar
barking
button

 **Read It Together** The artist has a party in her garden.

PM6.6

Unit 6 | Better Together

Name _____ Date _____

Lost and Found

Write a word from the box to complete each sentence.

High Frequency Words
another
began
buy
children
found
get
just
old
school
together

Mark and Lars were walking home from

school _____. They _____ a lost dog.

The dog was not old. It was _____ a

puppy. The dog _____ to follow them home. The

children saw one sign and then _____ one. The signs

said "Lost Puppy."

"When we _____ home, Mom can call these people

on the phone," Mark said.

"Maybe Mom can _____ us a puppy to keep!"

Lars exclaimed.

Name _____ Date _____

Mix and Match Sentences

Read a sentence in column A. Then draw a line to a word in column B that can replace the underlined part of the sentence. Have your partner say the sentence using the word from column B. Take turns drawing a line and saying the sentence. You can use the words in column B more than once.

A	B
<u>Mr. Adams</u> cuts the grass.	he
Give the shovel to <u>the girl</u>.	
<u>Mrs. Adams</u> is a good gardener.	she
<u>That tree</u> is huge!	
Walk to the garden with <u>your sister</u>.	it
Is <u>David</u> raking the leaves now?	
Help Mr. Adams with <u>that heavy bag</u>.	we
Do <u>your parents</u> like gardening?	
Give <u>the bag</u> to the boys.	they
Gardening is fun for <u>my brother</u>.	
<u>Aunt June and I</u> will plant some seeds.	him
Hand <u>this watering can</u> to Aunt June.	
Don't stand under <u>that tree</u> in a lightning storm.	her

Name _____ Date _____

Longer Words with *ar*

Write the word that completes each sentence.

1. arctic   cartoons   postmarks

Sometimes on weekends, Tess watches _____ on TV.

2. barnyard   yardstick   charcoal

One of them is about pigs in a _____.

3. scarlet   armhole   harvest

Once, the pigs got into the farm's _____.

4. margin   backyard   parsley

They ate all the parsnips and _____!

5. farmhand   starlight   carpet

A _____ had to chase the pigs away.

6. barbell   partway   army

When he was _____ across the yard, he slipped and fell in some mud. He could not get up.

7. hardship   cargo   farmer

The _____ came to help him, but it was hard and he slipped, too.

8. party   market   artist

The pigs watched and squealed. Did they think it was a funny mud _____? The farmers thought it was funny. Tess did, too.

Grammar and Writing

Write Pronouns

Read the story. Then choose the word from the box that correctly replaces the underlined word or words in each sentence.

I	he	him	her	it	we

Dad and I like to bake things. Dad and I ___We___

are making bread today. I hand Dad _____ the

flour from the cupboard. He mixes the flour _____

with water, salt, and yeast. Dad says, "This bread will

taste great to Mom, you, and me _____, won't it?"

Then Dad _____ kneads the bread for ten minutes.

Dad pops the bread into the oven. Dad says, "Dad

_____ didn't tell Mom we would be baking today."

"I want to surprise Mom _____."

Name _____ Date _____

Domino Soup

Make a story map for "Domino Soup."

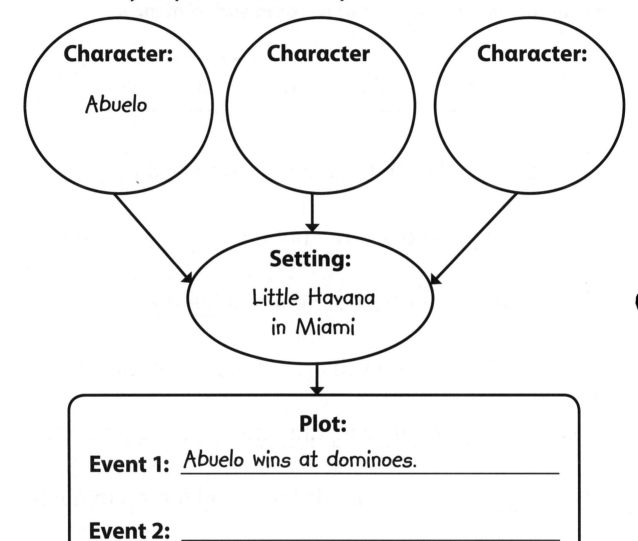

Character: Abuelo

Character

Character:

Setting: Little Havana in Miami

Plot:

Event 1: Abuelo wins at dominoes. _____

Event 2: _____

Event 3: _____

Event 4: _____

Share your story map with a partner. Compare the story elements you found for "Domino Soup."

Name _____ Date _____

Phonics

Words with *or, ore*

Unscramble each word and write it. Then write a sentence using the word.

1. o h n r	2. e t o r
<u>h</u> <u>o</u> <u>r</u> <u>n</u> I play the horn in a band.	__ __ __ __ _____
3. c n r o	**4. r f o t**
__ __ __ __ _____ _____	__ __ __ __ _____ _____
5. h r c e o	**6. r s o h t**
__ __ __ __ __ _____ _____	__ __ __ __ __ __ _____ _____
7. e n s r o	**8. o c r h p**
__ __ __ __ __ _____ _____	__ __ __ __ __ _____ _____

Name _____ Date _____

Words with *or, ore*

Write the words to complete each sentence.

1. chores   Mort

What does _____ do when he finishes his _____?

2. porch   sports

He sits on his _____ and watches a _____ game on TV.

3. more   score

He is hoping that his team will _____ some _____ runs.

4. horse   snort

Then he hears a _____ from his _____ in the barn.

5. north   storm

He looks up and sees a big _____ coming from the _____.

6. store   torch

He runs to the _____ to buy a _____ and some other supplies.

7. forth   shore

He sees sand whipping back and _____ by the _____.

8. force   before

Mort is glad to be safely at home _____ the full _____ of the storm hits!

● Word Cards: Words with *or, ore*

horse	chore	core	shore
sports	tore	sore	or
bore	force	stork	more
wore	corn	for	yore
nor	pork	snore	port
sort	spore	torn	ore
store	porch	born	score

horse	cart	store	person
		core	
	more		
	for	fort	worn
		fork	port
	chore	barn	form
store	porch	born	corn

● High Frequency Word Cards

family	line
mountain	done
every	side
blue	try
● only	once
first	must
fall	next
many	funny
most	follow
● also	laugh

Name _____ Date _____

Compare Two Versions of the Same Story

Use the comparison chart to show how "Domino Soup" and "Stone Soup" are alike and different.

	"Domino Soup"	"Stone Soup"
Type of Story	play	song
Characters		
Setting		
Plot		

 Tell a partner how the two versions of the story are the same and different.

Phonics

Longer Words with *or, ore*

Circle the word that names the picture.

1. (porthole) proceed provide	2. thanking tardy thorny	3. before blanket boring
4. forecast forest fastest	5. acorn accuse adore	6. porridge porthole popcorn
7. motor market morning	8. carport corncob cactus	9. horseback hornet harness
10. **40** forty forgive favor	11. odor organ orphan	12. snowstorm snorkel snoring

Read It Together We saw acorns and hornets in the forest this morning.

Name _____ Date _____

This Way or That Way?

Write a word from the box to complete each sentence.

High Frequency Words
done
follow
funny
laugh
line
must
next
once
side
try

1. I am in a _____ play at school.

2. I stand at the end of a long _____ of actors.

3. I _____ follow them and do what they do.

4. They all run to one _____ of the stage, but I run the other way.

5. That makes all the people _____ really hard!

6. I try again, but the _____ time they run left, and I run right!

7. Once the play is _____, the people say that they laughed at me the most.

Name _____ Date _____

Use Subject and Object Pronouns

Directions:

1. Make a spinner.

2. Play with a partner.

3. Take turns spinning the spinner.

4. Say a sentence using one of the words you landed on. Then have your partner say a sentence using the other word you landed on.

Make a Spinner
1. Put a paper clip ⌒ in the center of the circle.
2. Hold one end of the paper clip with a pencil.
3. Spin the paper clip around the pencil.

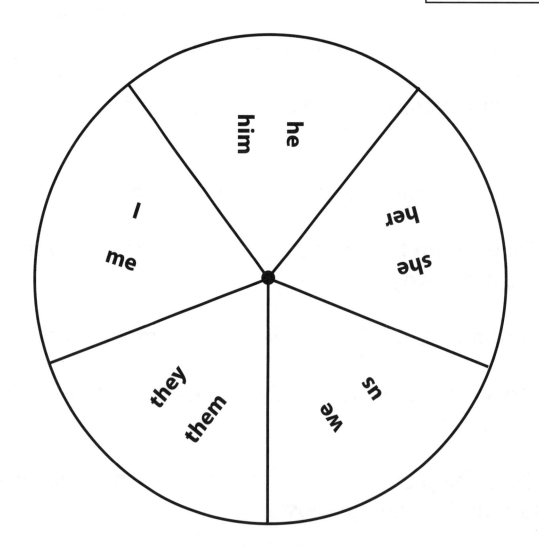

Name _____ Date _____

Longer Words with *or, ore*

Write the word that completes each sentence.

1. seashore   hornet   effort

Tory is at the _____ with her family.

2. pitchfork   porridge   explore

She wants to _____ the beach and look for fish in the water.

3. export   forecast   favor

She wakes up in the morning, but the _____ is for rain.

4. northwest   stormy   morning

It might get too _____ to be on the beach!

5. forest   ignore   boring

What will Tory do? It is _____ to stay inside the cabin!

6. popcorn   thorny   adore

"I know!" says Dad. "We can play games and eat _____."

7. forgets   before   orphan

Tory has so much fun that she _____ all about the rainstorm.

8. corncob   odor   report

The next morning, the _____ is for a hot, sunny day.

9. snorkel   organ   porthole

Tory goes to the beach with her _____. Which fish will she see?

Grammar and Writing

Write Subject and Object Pronouns

Read the story. Then choose the word from the box that correctly completes each sentence.

me	her	she	them	they	us

I love my grandmother. Having Grandma over

for supper is a lot of fun for ___*me*___. Grandma

looked hungry when _____ sat down at the table.

Mom, Dad, and I all smiled at her, and she smiled

back at _____. I said, "We picked the tomatoes

for the soup in our garden. _____ were really red

and ripe." Grandma answered, "Yes, I know. I saw

_____ sitting on the windowsill this afternoon."

Mom asked Grandma to pass the muffins to

_____. We had a great meal.

Grammar: Pronouns

Use Pronouns

Directions:

1. Play with a partner.

2. Spin the spinner.

3. Name a pronoun to replace the words in the space.

4. Say a sentence using the pronoun.

5. Color in the space.

6. Play until all the spaces are colored in.

Make a Spinner

1. Put a paper clip ⬭ in the center of the circle.

2. Hold one end of the paper clip with a pencil.

3. Spin the paper clip around the pencil.

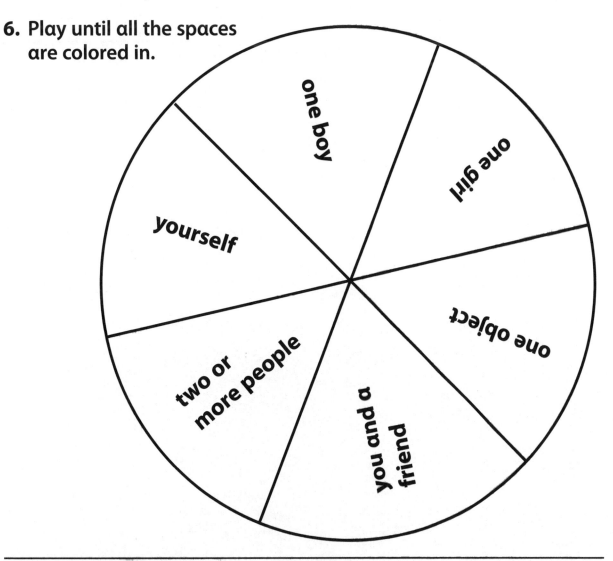

Words with *er, ir, ur*

Cut out the words and mix them up. Then sort them by *er*, *ir*, and *ur* spellings.

fern	**first**
her	**third**
herd	**burn**
perch	**burst**
birch	**church**
bird	**fur**

Name _____ Date _____

Main Idea

Make a main idea diagram to tell about a time you worked with someone to reach a goal.

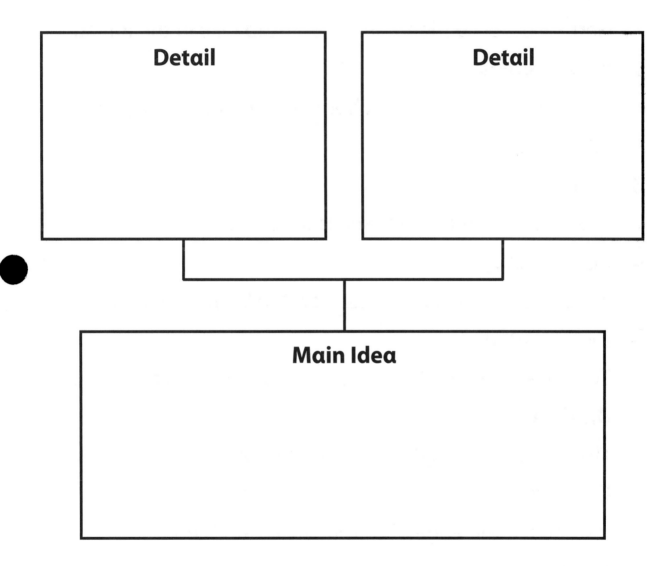

 Share your main idea diagram with a partner.

Name _____ Date _____

Phonics

Words with *er, ir, ur*

Write the words on the line to complete each sentence.

1. hers   urges

Gert _____ a friend of _____ to hike in the forest.

2. Kurt   serves

"The forest _____ as a home to a lot of wildlife," she

tells _____.

3. first   bird

The _____ thing they see is a _____.

4. perch   chirps

It _____ from its _____ on the branch of a tree.

5. fern   curled

Then they see a snake _____ around a green _____.

6. third   fur

The _____ thing they see is a fox with red _____.

7. fir   turns

It stands at the edge of a small field and then _____

and trots between two _____ trees.

8. curve   birch

The pals walk around a _____ in the path and pass a

white _____ tree as they walk out of the forest.

● Word Cards: Words with *er, ir, ur*

shirt	bird	mother	curl
squirm	serve	third	herd
fir	term	girl	dirt
nerve	her	flirt	after
father	birth	burn	nurse
fur	sir	hurt	surf
turn	sister	squirt	spurt

● High Frequency Word Cards

watch	boy
while	us
goes	pull
above	gave
● talk	took
long	myself
far	upon
something	brother
better	sister
● full	always

Name _____ Date _____

Longer Words with *er, ir, ur*

Circle the word that names the picture.

1. ruler / rubber / (river)	**2.** squirting / summer / squirrel	**3.** **13** thirteen / thirsty / Thursday
4. tiger / turkey / termite	**5.** spider / spurted / survive	**6.** city / sister / circus
7. teacher / turnip / thirty	**8.** burger / bigger / birthday	**9.** gerbil / giraffe / gopher
10. lurching / letter / lobster	**11.** perfume / paper / perfect	**12.** farmer / furry / firsthand

 **Read It Together** Are turkeys, spiders, lobsters, or squirrels furry?

Name _____ Date _____

Tugging Rope

Write a word from the box to complete each sentence.

High Frequency Words
always
boy
brother
gave
myself
pull
sister
took
upon
us

1. "I want to play a game," said the boy,

   "but I can't play by _____."

2. "I'll ask my brother, my _____, and my friends."

3. One team _____ one end of a rope, and one team grabbed the other end.

4. All the kids started to _____ hard.

5. One team _____ a really hard tug!

6. All the kids fell _____ the grass!

7. "We always fall when you tug hard," exclaimed the boy,

   "but you always fall with _____!"

Name _____ Date _____

Use Possessive Pronouns

Directions:

1. Make a spinner.

2. Play with a partner.

3. Take turns spinning the spinner.

4. Read the word. Say a sentence using the possessive pronoun you landed on. Then have your partner say another sentence using the same possessive pronoun.

Make a Spinner

1. Put a paper clip ⊂▭⊃ in the center of the circle.

2. Hold one end of the paper clip with a pencil.

3. Spin the paper clip around the pencil.

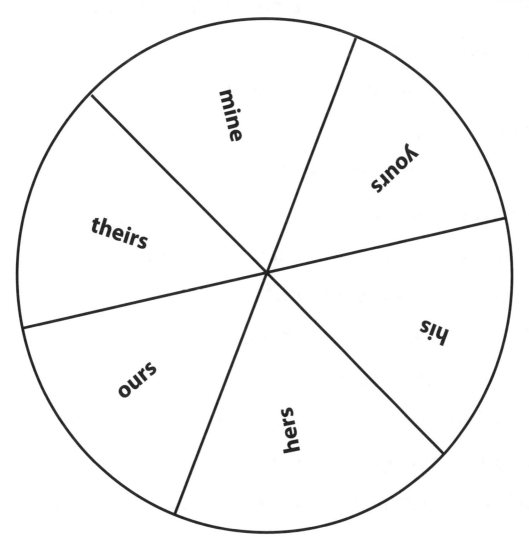

Name _____ Date _____

Longer Words with *er, ir, ur*

Write the word that completes each sentence.

1. crater   blurry   perfect

Shirley thinks that her two pet gerbils are _____ pets.

2. birthday   ladder   murmur

They were a _____ gift from her mom and dad.

3. surprised   winter   person

Shirley was _____ and happy when she got them!

4. painter   desert   herself

She found out that gerbils come from the _____.

5. after   Thursday   thirsty

That's why they don't get too _____.

6. survive   blurry   sternly

They can _____ without a lot of water!

7. hamsters   numbers   dirty

Some people confuse gerbils and _____.

8. furry   thirty   perform

Gerbils are the ones that have long, _____ tails.

9. pepper   turnip   chirping

When they are happy, they make _____ sounds.

Write Possessive Pronouns

Read the letter. Then choose the word from the box that correctly completes each sentence.

mine	yours	his	hers	ours	theirs

Hello.

    My name is Pencho Ragbey and I live in Tibet. I want to tell you about a special project of ___*ours*___. Our life in Tibet is very different from _____ in the United States. Here, many children do not go to school. _____ is a hard life of farming and herding.

    But this is changing. We worked together to build a school for our village. My sister Tsering helped start a group. The idea for the group was _____. One of my teachers helps us learn to use a computer. The first computer at school was _____, but now we have others. I am writing to you on a new computer. This one is _____!

                              Sincerely,
                              Pencho Ragbey

Apply Word Knowledge

Vocabulary Bingo

Key Words	
dream	plan
education	project
join	result
opportunity	skills
organize	success

1. **Write one Key Word in each school.**

2. **Listen to the clues. Find the Key Word and color it in.**

3. **Say "Bingo" when you have four markers in a row.**

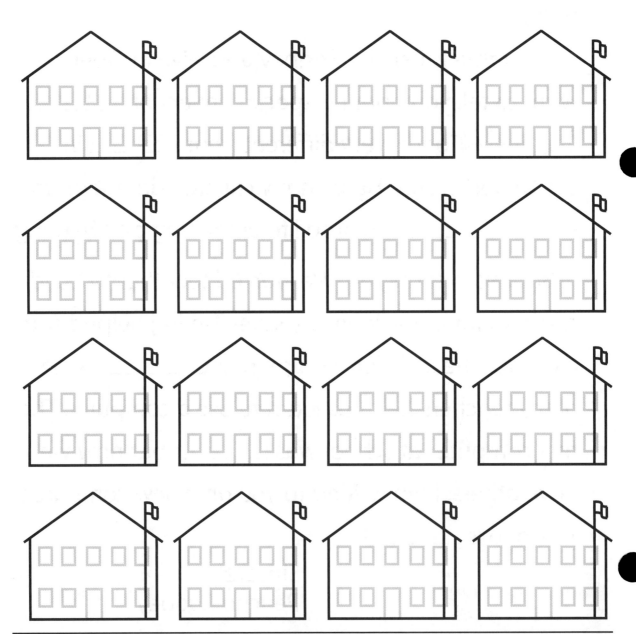

Name _____ Date _____

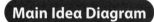

In a Mountain Community

Make a main idea diagram for "In a Mountain Community."

Detail	**Detail**
The people of Chungba raise money for a school.	

Main Idea

 Share your main idea diagram with a partner. See if you found the same main idea.

Phonics

Words with *air, are, ear*

Circle the word that names the picture.

1.	2.	3.
bake (bear) blare	squeak squirt square	sharp share shore
4.	**5.**	**6.**
peer pore pear	chase chair chain	spread spare spark
7.	**8.**	**9.**
fare far frame	hard hare hurt	pay peak pair
10.	**11.**	**12.**
pare park part	air aim awake	hair hear her

Read It Together   We saw a pair of hares share some grass.

PM6.35

Name _____ Date _____

Phonics

Words with *air, are, ear*

Write the words to complete each sentence.

1. chair   airplane

Vic falls asleep in his _____ on the _____.

2. scary   nightmare

He has a _____ that is _____.

3. hair   stare

First, people _____ at him because his _____ is green.

4. pear   mare

Next, a hungry _____ chases him because she wants

to eat his _____.

5. scare   bear

Then he gets an even bigger _____ when a furry

_____ chases him up a tree!

6. hares   fair

Then, he is at a _____ and sees two huge _____.

7. pair   rare

It is a _____ sight to see the _____ chasing him!

8. staircase   daring

Vic makes a _____ escape up a _____.

● Word Cards: Words with *air, are, ear*

chair	airplane	hare	bear
stair	lair	mare	hairy
share	care	rare	glare
pear	hair	stare	pair
air	wear	fairy	bare
fair	scare	dare	dairy
tear	spare	swear	fare

● High Frequency Word Cards

almost	made
again	five
tomorrow	four
between	men
● went	night
surprise	such
never	well
any	wish
grow	second
● below	thought

Comparison Chart

Compare Texts

Use the comparison chart to show how "In a Mountain Community" and "Mi Barrio" are alike and different.

	"In a Mountain Community"	"Mi Barrio"
It is in an urban community.		✓
It is in a rural community.	✓	
The community members help each other.		
The children help their community, too.		
The selection is illustrated with photographs.		
It is a true story.		

 Compare your chart with a partner's. See if you found the same information.

Phonics

Words with *eer, ear*

Circle the word that names the picture.

1. (deer) dare deeper	**2.** air ore ear	**3.** tire tear tore
4. spear speak seal	**5.** hair hear heat	**6.** store street steer
7. beard bored bird	**8.** fear farm fair	**9.** stars stirs stairs
10. chirp cheer cheap	**11.** bar bore bear	**12.** peak peer plea

Read It Together A deer uses its ears to hear sounds in the forest.

Name _____ Date _____

Wish Upon a Star

Write a word from the box to complete each sentence.

High Frequency Words
five
four
made
men
night
second
such
thought
well
wish

Dear Grandpa,

I camped in a tent last _____. I

_____ it would be scary, but it was

_____ fun! Dad told me about _____ who

studied the stars a long time ago. I could see four

or _____ stars in the sky really well. I made a

_____ upon one of them! Then I made a _____

one. I wished you could be here with us!

Your grandson,

Marcus

Grammar: Pronouns

Mix and Match Sentences

First choose a word or words from column A. Then choose a word from column B. Say a sentence using both parts and any other words you want to add. You may have to change the form of some of the words. After you say your sentence, have your partner replace the noun you chose with a pronoun and say the new sentence.

A	B
Ms. White	hat
The dogs	foot
A big tree	bike
The police officer's	house
Michael's	phone
A book	roar
A computer	gloves
A girl	coat
A man	car
Dad's	leaves
A lion	tail
The fish	head
A friend's	cover
Mom's	screen

Name _____ Date _____

Longer Words with *eer, ear*

Write the word that completes each sentence.

1. nearby   yearly   sneering

My class went on a field trip to a _____ farm.

2. dreary   gears   shearing

First, we saw a farmer _____ some sheep.

3. sheer   earmuffs   dearly

I could hear sheep bleating, even with my _____ on!

4. steer   clear   bleary

Next, we saw a big _____ in a field.

5. wheelchair   peering   spear

When it looked up, I thought it was _____ at me!

6. smear   eerie   earring

I thought that was sort of _____!

7. cheery   earlobe   rearing

We saw a horse _____ up on its back legs.

8. veer   fear   nearly

Another horse had to _____ out of the way!

9. deer   weary   beard

We walked so much that I was _____ at the end of the day.

Name _____   Date _____

Grammar and Writing

Write Pronouns

Read the story. Then choose the word from the box that correctly completes each sentence.

I	she	him	us	his	herself

Some kids in Amber's class want to learn about the neighborhood. Amber tells __herself__ that she knows whom they should see to learn about the neighborhood. _____ suggests they talk to Mr. Sanchez. The kids go to see _____ at his store. Amber opens the door and says, "Here we go. This store is _____." They ask Mr. Sanchez about all his memories of the neighborhood. "_____ am so glad you talked about the neighborhood," Amber says. "Thank you so much for talking to _____."

Name _____ Date _____

Use Possessive Pronouns

Directions:

1. Play with two or three people. Copy all the words below onto separate cards.

2. Mix the cards up and put them facedown.

3. Turn over two cards and read them aloud. If the possessive pronoun card matches the noun card, keep both cards. If the two cards do not match, turn them facedown again in the same place.

4. The player with the most cards at the end wins.

Nouns			
Lee and Ana's notes	Our project	Lupe's and your plans	Lilu's marker
My goals	Your skill	Jackson's paper	

Possessive Pronouns			
Mine	Yours	Ours	Theirs
His	Hers	Yours	

 Use three of the nouns above. Tell a partner something about yourself.

Phonics

Prefixes *un-, re-, mis-*

Circle the word that names the picture.

1. mistreat (refill) unfilled	**2.** unhappy retied misread	**3.** deg dog unpack relock misspell
4. mismatch rematch unkind	**5.** unload mislead replace	**7.** misname resealed unsealed
7. mistake unmade remake	**8.** undo reset misuse	**9.** replay unkind misplace
10. untied retied mistied	**11.** misstep unsafe rewrap	**12.** unfolds refolded mistrust

Read It Together Mom is unhappy and replaces my mismatched socks.

Name _____ Date _____

Characters' Motives

Make a character map for the animal in your story.

Character	What the Character Does	What the Character is Like

 Tell a partner your story. Then share your character map. Talk about the character's motives.

Phonics

Prefixes *un-, re-, mis-*

Write the word that completes each sentence.

1. rename   misuse   unlike

My dog's name is Lucky, but I should _____ him Unlucky!

2. unpaid   reheated   misjudged

Once he tried to jump over a stream, but he _____ his jump and landed with a big splash!

3. rereads   misplaces   unties

He likes to play fetch, but he often _____ his stick.

4. retrace   misuse   unzip

Then he has to _____ his steps until he finds it.

5. misread   refill   unwise

Once Lucky was not very smart and did something that was

_____.

6. unfair   mistake   recall

He made a big _____ when he tried to play with a skunk.

7. unfold   misspell   rewash

We gave him a bath and then had to _____ him for days!

8. rewind   unhappy   misstep

He was _____ because he hates baths!

● Word Cards: Words with *un-, re-, mis-*

unplug	**refill**	**remail**	**mismatch**
mistreat	mistake	unseen	undo
unsafe	unwanted	resave	mistrust
rename	retake	unheard	unwind
misbehave	misread	restate	reawake
unhurt	misjudge	resend	misprint
revote	unasked	misspell	redo

● High Frequency Word Cards

get	move
buy	ball
old	few
just	eye
● school	food
children	large
found	number
began	animal
another	often
● together	might

Name _____ Date _____

Suffixes -y, -ly, -ful

Circle the word that names the picture.

1. carry / careless / (careful)	**2.** muddy / mindful / mostly	**3.** closely / curly / cheerful
4. loudly / lefty / lapful	**5.** cupful / quickly / quirky	**7.** highly / hungry / helpful
7. thickly / thankful / thirsty	**8.** playful / picky / partly	**9.** softly / sandy / forceful
10. gently / graceful / grumpy	**11.** windy / wisely / wishful	**12.** skillful / sleepy / slowly

Read It Together   My fluffy, playful kitten mews loudly.

Name _____ Date _____

Helping Out

Write a word from the box to complete each sentence.

High Frequency **Words**
animal
ball
eye
few
food
large
might
move
number
often

Dear Pedro,

I _____ be home late. Please help

Grandma when you get home. First, feed

each _____. The dog gets three large scoops of

_____. The cat gets a different _____. She gets

only one. Then take the dog outside. Throw a _____

a few times for the dog to fetch. Be careful that the

cat doesn't get out the door. Keep your eye on her. She

_____ sneaks out, and she can _____ fast!

Thank you,

Mom

● Word Cards: Past Tense

add -*ed*	double consonant and add -*ed*	drop final silent *e* and add -*ed*	change *y* to *i* and add -*ed*
carry	dare	ask	like
water	watch	study	soak
grab	serve	check	show
try	use	snap	care
stop	move	worry	rub
pull	copy	surprise	hop

For use with TE p. T403n   **PM7.8**   **Unit 7** | Best Buddies

Name _____ Date _____

Suffixes -y, -ly, -ful

Write the word with the correct suffix to complete each sentence.

1. wind

On a _____ day, Kelly flies her kite.

2. grace

She watches her _____ kite float through the sky.

3. quick

It swoops down _____ before it sails back up high.

4. snow

On a _____ day, Kelly goes sledding.

5. care

She is _____ on the hills.

6. safe

She sleds _____ where there are no trees.

7. rain

On a _____ day, Kelly stays inside.

8. close

She watches the rain _____.

9. hope

Kelly is _____ that the rain will stop soon so she can go outside to play.

Grammar and Writing

Write Past-Tense Verbs

Read the story. Then choose the word from the word box that correctly completes each sentence. Write its past-tense form on the blank.

ask	copy	grab	like	show	worry

Yesterday, I _____asked_____ my uncle to help me make

a birdhouse. He _____ his tool kit and came right

over. I showed him my drawing that I _____ from

a book. First, we got some wood. Then he _____

me how to measure the pieces. I _____ that I

could not cut the pieces straight, so he cut them for

me. Soon, the birdhouse was finished. We both really

_____ the new birdhouse.

Name _____ Date _____

Go to Sleep, Gecko!

Make a character map for the characters in "Go to Sleep, Gecko!"

Character	What the Character Does	What the Character is Like
Gecko	He complains about the fireflies.	He can't sleep.

 Share your character map with a partner. Compare what you wrote about the characters in "Go to Sleep, Gecko!"

Name _____ Date _____

Phonics

Words with *oo, ea, ou*

Cut out the words and sort them. Use the words in sentences.

wood	**feather**
took	**weather**
stood	**steady**
brook	**touch**
cookie	**young**
breath	**cousin**

Name _____ Date _____

Words with *oo, ea, ou*

Write the words to complete each sentence.

1. cook   young

Dad started to _____ when he was a _____ boy.

2. cookbooks   read

He _____ Grandma's _____ and chose things
to make.

3. look   books

Now other people _____ for food to make in _____
that Dad writes.

4. instead   breakfast

Sometimes Dad makes eggs for _____, but this morning

he made oatmeal _____.

5. good   bread

He made some _____ that was really _____, too.

6. cousin   took

First I _____ a taste, and then my _____ did.

7. shook   head

He _____ his _____, patted his tummy, and said,
"Yum!"

Phonics

Words with *gh*

Unscramble each word and write it. Then write a sentence using the word.

1. g o r u h _r_ _o_ _u_ _g_ _h_ This sand feels rough.	**2. t g t i h** _ _ _ _ _
3. h a g s n _ _ _ _ _	**4. u h t o g** _ _ _ _ _
5. h e u n o g _ _ _ _ _ _	**7. r g b i h t** _ _ _ _ _ _
7. y r h g l u o _ _ _ _ _ _ _	**8. s g i i h g n** _ _ _ _ _ _ _

● Word Cards: Words with *oo, ea, ou*

cookie	book	bread	couple
young	enough	read	look
notebook	cousin	rookie	dead
rough	rook	touch	double
thread	health	hook	meadow
cook	shook	instead	nook
head	country	trouble	tough

● High Frequency Word Cards

line	room
done	head
side	small
try	pick
● once	own
must	stay
next	along
funny	change
follow	sometimes
● laugh	enough

For use with TE p. T429g **PM7.16** Unit 7 | Best Buddies

Compare Genres

Complete the comparison chart to show how the selections are the same and different.

"Go to Sleep, Gecko!"	"Enric Sala: Marine Ecologist"
• folk tale • fiction	• folk tale • fiction

 Use your comparison chart to tell a partner how "Go to Sleep, Gecko!" and "Enric Sala: Marine Ecologist" are alike and different.

Phonics

Words with *au, aw*

Circle the word that names the picture.

1. sea (saw) sat	2. line lawn loan	3. ray raw row
4. claw clap clear	**5.** pen paw pea	**6.** jaw jam jug
7. deep draw dad	**8.** hike hawk heat	**9.** lump lawn lamp
10. road raw rod	**11.** pie pin prawn	**12.** crawl crane crow

Read It Together Paul and his dog saw a hawk along the road.

High Frequency Words

Watch Them Grow!

Write a word from the box to complete each sentence.

High Frequency **Words**
along
change
enough
head
own
pick
room
small
sometimes
stay

1. We have just _____ room to have two pear trees in the backyard.

2. The trees are still _____, but pears grow on them.

3. I like to watch the pears get bigger and _____ as they grow.

4. Most of the pears _____ on the branches, but sometimes they fall.

5. Once a ripe yellow pear fell and hit me right on the top of my _____!

6. I like it when the end of summer comes _____.

7. Then I can _____ my own pears to eat!

Grammar: Irregular Past-Tense Verbs

Use Irregular Verbs

1. To play, take turns with a partner.
2. Toss a marker onto the game board.
3. Say a sentence with the present-tense verb you land on. Then say the past-tense verb and use it in a sentence to tell about the past.

do	go
says	sing
give	takes

Phonics

Words with *au, aw*

Write the words to complete each sentence.

1. yawned   dawn

Mai woke up at _____ and _____.

2. saw   fawn

She looked outside and _____ a _____.

3. lawn   tawny

The _____ animal was eating weeds on her _____.

4. sauntered   paused

When Mai went outside, the animal _____ and then

_____ back into the woods.

5. claws   hawk

Mai saw a _____ swoop down and grab food in its

_____.

6. launched   hauled

Then it _____ itself back up into the sky and _____
its food away.

7. because   draw

Mai ran back inside _____ she wanted to _____
the animals.

Grammar and Writing

Write Irregular Verbs

Read the letter. Then write the word from the word box that correctly completes each sentence.

begin	come	do	give	go
began	came	did	gave	went

Dear Grandpa,

This is what we ___did___ in school last week. Every

kid decided to be an animal. Then we each _____

a talk about the animal we were. We all _____

turns telling about ourselves. My friend Sarah

_____ first. She was a penguin. She was great. She

_____ to talk about all the raw fish she liked to

eat. Then my turn _____. I was a tiger!

Love,

Marike

Name _____ Date _____

Use Past-Tense Verbs

Grammar Rules Past-Tense Verbs

- Add *-ed* to most verbs when you talk about a past action. Example: *kick* + *-ed* = *kicked*

- Some verbs have special forms to show an action in the past. Example: *say* ➔ *said*

Circle the correct verb form.

1. Gecko want/(wanted) to sleep that night.

2. Gecko goed/went to see Elephant.

3. Elephant talks/talked to the fireflies last week.

4. The fireflies seed/saw Elephant coming.

5. Gecko sayed/said everything was okay.

 Use the past tense of *is* or *are* in a sentence about Gecko.

_____

Phonics

Words with *al, all*

Circle the word that names the picture.

1.
tell
tail
(tall)

2.
hill
hall
heel

3.
will
wall
well

4.
bald
bold
bell

5.
bell
bill
ball

6.
fall
fill
feel

7.
small
smell
smile

8.
sale
salt
seal

9.
stair
store
steer

10.
hail
heel
hill

11.
cool
call
curl

12.
hall
hat
heat

Read It Together Walk by the tall wall. Did the ball fall there?

Name _____ Date _____

Topic and Main Idea

Work with a partner. What nonfiction selection have you both read? Find the topic and main idea of the selection. Then fill out the chart.

Topic	Main Idea

 Use your chart to discuss the topic and main idea of your selection.

For use with TE p. T439a   **PM7.25**   Unit 7 | Best Buddies

Phonics

Words with *al, all*

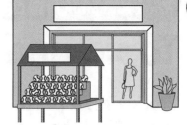

Write the words to complete each sentence.

1. mall   Hall

Mrs. _____ and her family took a trip to the _____.

2. stalls   hallway

People were selling goods from _____ in the _____.

3. baseballs   bald

A _____ man was selling _____.

4. ball   always

Billy _____ wanted to have his very own _____.

5. wallet   almost

He looked in his _____ and saw that he had _____ enough cash.

6. all   tallest

His _____ sister looked at _____ her cash.

7. smallest   also

His _____ sister _____ looked in her purse.

8. baseball   all

Together, they had _____ the cash Billy needed to get a

new _____!

● Word Cards: Words with *al, all*

salt	bald	ball	almond
Walt	basket-ball	mall	football
hallway	almost	wall	always
tall	fall	scald	hallway
salty	halt	squalls	volleyball
small	call	stall	waltz
false	malted	also	alter

● # High Frequency Word Cards

boy	ride
us	close
pull	sleep
gave	cry
● took	show
myself	green
upon	plant
brother	hurt
sister	jump
● always	please

Name _____ Date _____

Words with *oi, oy*

Circle the word that names the picture.

1. corn / (coin) / cone	**2.** oil / old / eel	**3.** pot / paint / point toy join
4. box / boy / bee	**5.** toy / tea / top	**7.** nose / noise / nice
7. teeth / toast / toys	**8.** boil / bake / book	**9.** vase / voice / vest
10. spoil / spot / speed	**11.** sail / soil / sell	**12.** coil / coat / cat

Read It Together   Point to the toys that make the most noise.

Name _____ Date _____

The Boat Ride

Write a word from the box to complete each sentence.

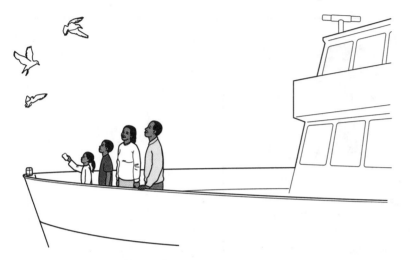

High Frequency **Words**
close
cry
green
hurt
jump
plant
please
ride
show
sleep

My family and I _____ to the beach

on a boat. Some gulls are flying _____

to the boat. I show them some bread, and

they _____ out. They seem to say, "Will you _____

share your bread with us?" I put bread on the railing

and step back. The gulls fly down. I jump, but they don't

_____ me. They just take the bread from the railing! I

sit in the sun, close my eyes, and go to _____. When I

wake up, I see a big _____ plant on the shoreline and

know that we are almost at the beach!

Name _____ Date _____

Use Future-Tense Verbs with *Will*

Directions:

1. Make a spinner.

2. Play with a partner.

3. Take turns spinning the spinner.

4. Read the words. Say a sentence using a contraction for the words you land on. Then have your partner say your sentence without the contraction.

Make a Spinner
1. Put a paper clip ⌷ in the center of the circle.
2. Hold one end of the paper clip with a pencil.
3. Spin the paper clip around the pencil.

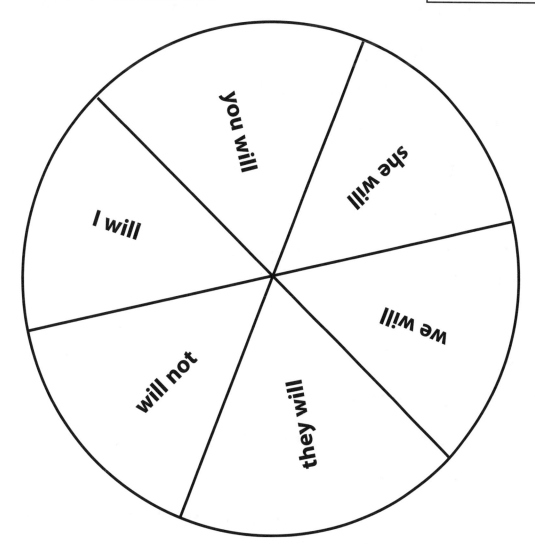

Name _____ Date _____

Words with *oi, oy*

Write the word that completes each sentence.

1. enjoy   newsboy   oil

What do you _____ doing on a hot day?

2. oyster   soil   voice

Joy plants seeds in the _____ in her garden.

3. royal   point   moist

She must keep the dirt _____ so the seeds will grow.

4. joins   joyful   loyal

Troy _____ his pals at the field in a nearby park.

5. spoil   sirloin   noisy

They play a _____ game of baseball.

6. toy   broiling   joint

When they get _____ hot, they jump into the swimming pool at the park.

7. soy   coil   choice

Roy makes a different _____.

8. boil   coins   noise

He takes some _____ from his piggybank.

9. boy   foil   pointing

Then the happy _____ rides his bike to the ice cream shop!

Name _____   Date _____

● **Grammar and Writing**

Write Future-Tense Verbs with *Will*

Read the story. Then choose the word from the word box that correctly completes each sentence.

he'll   it'll   we'll   I'll   won't   they'll

Our class is going to the zoo. I am sure ___*we'll*___

have a fantastic time. I love the monkeys. I hope

_____ do lots of funny things. Mr. Dean, our

teacher, says _____ tell us about the different

animals. I hope the weather is good. _____ be

great if the sun shines. It _____ be as good if it

rains, but the zoo trip will still be fun. _____ tell

you all about it!

Vocabulary

Yes or No?

> 1. Listen to the questions. Write the Key Word where it belongs in each sentence.
>
> 2. Listen to the questions again.
>
> 3. Write <u>yes</u> or <u>no</u> for each question.

1. Do animals in the wild hide from ___danger___ ? ___yes___

2. Are cleaner shrimp and oxpeckers animal _____ ?

_____

3. Can animals _____ each other? _____

4. Is a plover _____ to a honeyguide bird? _____

5. Are the clownfish and sea anemone _____ partners?

_____

6. Does a badger have the _____ to help a coyote?

_____

Name _____ Date _____

Odd Couples

FIll out the topic and main idea chart for "Odd Couples."

Topic:	Main Idea: Animal partnerships help both animals survive.

Detail:
Cleaner shrimp keep other fish clean.

Detail:

 Use your topic and main idea chart to tell a partner about "Odd Couples."

Name _____   Date _____

Words with *ow, ou*

Unscramble each word and write it. Then write a sentence using the word.

1. o l u d <u>l o u d</u> <u>I hear a loud noise.</u> _____	**2. o n d w** _ _ _ _ _____ _____
3. w l h o _ _ _ _ _____ _____	**4. d l c u o** _ _ _ _ _ _____ _____
5. t u c o n _ _ _ _ _ _ _____ _____	**6. d w o c r** _ _ _ _ _ _____ _____
7. n f w r o _ _ _ _ _ _____ _____	**8. o g n u r d** _ _ _ _ _ _ _____ _____

Name _____ Date _____

Words with *ow, ou*

Write the words to complete each sentence.

1. now   downtown

Right _____ Dad and I are _____ at the circus.

2. surrounds   round

A big, _____ tent _____ us.

3. crowd   shouts

The _____ claps and _____ at all the circus acts.

4. frown   clown

I like the funny _____ with a huge, red _____ for a mouth.

5. cowboy   flower

He wears a _____ hat with a red _____ on top.

6. hound   crouches

He _____ down low and pretends to be a _____ that is howling.

7. brown   crowns

Dad likes the _____ horses wearing _____ on their heads.

8. thousand   drowsy

By the end, I am _____, but I wish I could come back a _____ more times!

● Word Cards: Words with *ou, ow*

hound	pound	tower	flower
count	pounce	found	towel
power	wow	howl	loud
under-ground	shower	sound	around
crowd	town	down	ground
hour	about	round	pout
frown	crowded	vow	downtown

For use with TE p. T459g   **PM7.38**   Unit 7 | Best Buddies

● High Frequency Word Cards

made	will
five	soon
four	black
men	brown
● night	group
such	high
well	leave
wish	study
second	open
● thought	point

For use with TE p. T459g   **PM7.39**   **Unit 7** | Best Buddies

Name _____ Date _____

Compare Topics and Main Ideas

Complete the comparison chart to compare "Odd Couples" and "Working Together."

Title	Topic	Main Idea
"Odd Couples"		
"Working Together"		

 Use the comparison chart to explain the topic and main idea of each selection.

Phonics

Words with Schwa

Circle the word that names the picture.

1. await abrupt (asleep)	2. alive ajar ago	3. along adult anew
4. amazed around amount	5. awake along awhile	6. aloud agree alone
7. avoid ashore ashes	8. afraid alert alike	9. alarm away alright
10. ahead appear adore	11. aware afoot afloat	12. account across annoy

Read It Together Are you awake or asleep after your alarm rings?

Name _____ Date _____

At the Lighthouse

Write a word from the box to complete each sentence.

High Frequency **Words**
black
brown
group
high
leave
open
point
soon
study
will

1. When you _____ the bus stop, turn left on the first street.

2. Walk to the _____ where Hill Street meets Rocky Road, and you will see a brown house with a black door.

3. Turn right, and _____ you will come to a lighthouse.

4. Walk up the stairs to the top, and you will be _____ above the world!

5. You can look out over the _____ sea!

6. You might see a _____ of sea birds fly by.

7. You can _____ these birds to find out about them.

● Word Cards: Future-Tense Verbs

tell	watch	eat	give
visit	hunt	make	see
need	fly	stop	start
study	swim	sit	leave
help	look	catch	use
clean	ride	play	stay
ask	give	walk	buy

Unit 7 | Best Buddies

Name _____ Date _____

Words with Schwa

Write the words to complete each sentence.

1. alarm   awake

I'm wide _____ when my _____ goes off.

2. awhile   across

I wait _____ and then run _____ the house to find
Mom and Dad.

3. asleep   appear

They _____ to be _____.

4. aloud   aware

So I yell _____, "Are you _____ of the time?"

5. about   annoyed

"It's only _____ seven o'clock, isn't it?" says Dad. He sounds
a little _____.

6. awaiting   away

It's later than that, and I've been _____ this day for a long
time. I don't go _____.

7. alone   agree

Finally I _____ to leave them _____ until nine.

8. adore   arrive

At ten o'clock, we _____ at the dog pound, and I choose
my new puppy. I _____ her!

Write Future-Tense Verbs

Read the email. Then choose the word or words from the box that correctly complete each sentence. Write the words.

will	is going	she's	are going	am	you're

Hey Jason,

I have got some cool news! My mom got a new job at the zoo. Mom __is going__ to start next month.

_____ going to be the new assistant beekeeper.

I _____ going to visit the zoo and learn all about the bees. Mom _____ show me how the bees make honey. Of course, _____ going to come with me. You and I _____ to have a great time at the zoo!

Pablo

Name _____ Date _____

Say Future-Tense Verbs

Directions:

1. Play with a partner.

2. Spin the spinner.

3. Change the verb to show the future tense. Say a sentence using the future-tense verb.

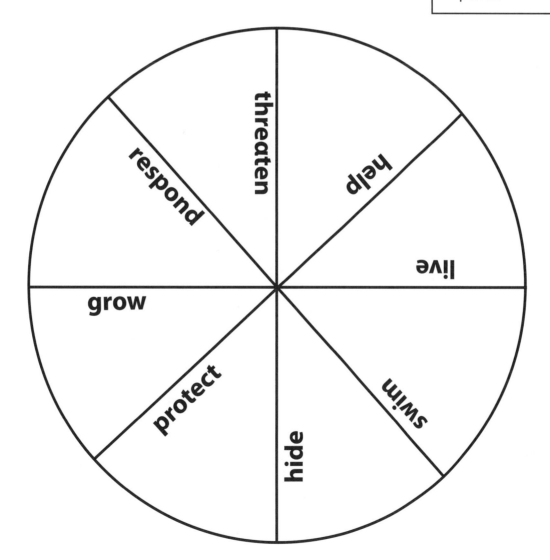

Phonics

Prefixes *dis-, pre-, in-, im-*

Cut out the cards. Match cards to make words. Then use each word in a sentence.

dis	teen
pre	heat
in	put
im	land
like	perfect
appear	polite

Name _____ Date _____

Characters' Feelings

Make a character map to tell how a character feels and why.

Character	How the Character Feels	Why the Character Feels This Way

 Use your character map to tell a partner about a character's feelings in a story that you like.

Name _____ Date _____

Prefixes *dis-, pre-, in-, im-*

Write the word that completes each sentence.

1. distrust   preschool   indoors

Cole and Rosa have to stay
_____ today because it is raining.

2. disagree   impolite   incomplete

At first they _____ about what
to do, but then they decide to make
cookies.

3. precut   incorrect   immigrate

Rosa thinks Cole likes peanut butter cookies, but she
is _____.

4. inputs   prepays   dislikes

Cole _____ peanut butter, so they decide to make
oatmeal cookies.

5. disarmed   pregame   imperfect

They don't want the cookies to be _____, so they work
carefully.

6. implant   preplan   insight

They _____ and prepare before they begin.

7. indirect   improper   disappear

After the cookies are baked, they _____ quickly! Yum!

● Words with Prefixes *dis-, pre-, im-, in-*

display	preschool	impossible	inside
disagree	disrespect	immature	inhuman
prepay	indecent	preview	immobile
impolite	disorder	imperfect	informal
disservice	improper	disapprove	prejudge
infield	incorrect	pregame	dissatisfied
precook	preorder	insecure	impatient

For use with TE p. T471k   **PM8.4**

● High Frequency Word Cards

move	seem
ball	word
few	read
eye	learn
● food	idea
large	father
number	mother
animal	country
often	picture
● might	America

Phonics

Suffixes -er, -or, -less, -ness

Circle the word that names the picture.

1. brainless brightness (baker)	**2.** farmer fearless fondness	**3.** trainer tractor truthless
4. darkness dancer dodger	**5.** hardness hunter hopeless	**7.** supper slowness swimmer
7. dryness doctor danger	**8.** sailor singer sadness	**9.** thicker thinker timeless
10. batter boneless blackness	**11.** spineless spotless speaker	**12.** kicker cordless kindness

Read It Together   The sailor is a fearless swimmer.

Name _____ Date _____

A New Home

Write a word from the box to complete each sentence.

Mom Me Dad

High Frequency **Words**
America
country
father
idea
learn
mother
picture
read
seem
word

Dear Grandma and Grandpa,

Here is a _____ of my father, my

mother, and me. We are in our new _____, the

United States of America. I _____ new things in

school every day. I can _____ in English now. I teach

myself at least one new English _____ every day.

I am happy, and Mom and Dad _____ happy, too.

I have a great _____! Can you come and visit us

soon? I miss you!

Your grandson,

Hector

● Word Cards: Prepositions

above	behind	in	in front of
at	beside	on	under
flag	door	parade	picnic
● lunch	sky	car	band
birthday	fireworks	party	food
milk	pie	table	customers
roof	window	chairs	horses
● people	house	street	float

Name _____ Date _____

Suffixes -er, -or, -less, -ness

Write the word that completes each sentence.

1. fondness   careless   tractor

Dale has a _____ for the sea.

2. helpless   brightness   sailor

That's why he wants to be a _____ when he grows up.

3. rancher   cloudless   actor

He wants to travel under _____ skies.

4. joyless   diver   dryness

Maybe he will also be a _____ who explores life under the water.

5. richness   painter   useless

He will learn about the _____ of life in the sea.

6. settler   visitor   darkness

Maybe he will study life in the _____ at the bottom.

7. cordless   teacher   lightless

It is _____ down where the sun doesn't shine!

8. worker   harmless   moistness

What kind of _____ would you like to be when you grow up?

9. greenness   hairless   countless

You have _____ jobs to choose from!

Grammar and Writing

Write Prepositions

Read the story. Then choose the word from the box that correctly completes each sentence.

above	behind	beside	in	on	under

I watched the Fourth of July parade last week. I watched it sitting _*beside*_ my parents. The parade was _____ Main Street. My sister plays in the high school band. The band marched _____ the parade. We waited for the band. The sky _____ us was very clear. I got really hot. Mom gave me a cold drink from the cooler _____ her chair. Then, we finally saw my sister. She was playing the trumpet. She was marching _____ a boy playing a drum.

For use with TE p. T471n   **PM8.10**

Name _____ Date _____

Apple Pie 4th of July

Make a character map for the characters in "Apple Pie 4th of July."

Character	How the Character Feels	Why the Character Feels This Way
The girl telling the story	Unhappy	She thinks no one will want Chinese food on the Fourth of July.

 Use your character map to describe the story characters to a partner.

Name _____   Date _____

Final Syllable Consonant + *le*

Circle the word that names the picture.

1. able (apple) anthill	**2.** candle candy cuddle	**3.** pebble paddle puzzle
4. bottle bottom bumble	**5.** needy nibble needle	**6.** bundle bunny bubble
7. tattle table trouble	**8.** cattle crackle cable	**9.** cradle circus circle
10. purple poodle puddle	**11.** little laundry lentil	**12.** turtle tunnel tangle

Read It Together   Would you put an apple or cattle on a table?

PM8.12

Name _____ Date _____

Final Syllable Consonant + *le*

Write the word that completes each sentence.

1. maples   riddles   giggles

Can you answer these _____?

2. turtle   cradle   sprinkle

I am a reptile, and I have a shell. I am a _____.

3. handle   gentle   poodle

I am a dog, and I have curly fur. I am a _____.

4. apple   uncle   eagle

I fly high in the sky because I am a bird. I am an _____.

5. beetle   title   noodle

I am a small bug with a shell. I am a _____.

6. fiddles   pebbles   wiggles

We are small rocks. We are _____.

7. rattle   bubble   saddle

You put me on a horse before you ride. I am a _____.

8. fizzle   jungle   gobble

I am where tigers and monkeys live. I am the _____.

9. purple   sparkle   cuddle

You get me if you mix red and blue paint. I am _____.

● Word Cards: Words with C + *le*

eagle	candle	turtle	puzzle
purple	middle	silly	finally
squeal	skillet	candy	stable
single	fable	let	pale
example	crate	maple	bridle
quilt	rifle	pellet	whale
rally	gentle	noble	steeple

● High Frequency Word Cards

room	got
head	tell
small	story
pick	sing
● own	song
stay	music
along	still
change	state
sometimes	today
● enough	example

High Frequency Word Cards

room

hear

small

pick

own

play

along

change

sometimes

enough

got

tell

story

sing

song

music

still

state

today

example

Comparison Chart

Compare Language

Compare the language in "Apple Pie 4th of July" and "America: A Weaving." Write what the sentences or phrases mean.

"Apple Pie 4th of July"	"America: A Weaving"
I hear the parade passing by. *This means exactly what it says.*	America, America, a never-ending weaving! *Meaning: Many cultures and traditions make America.*
My parents do not understand all American things.	

 Take turns with a partner. Explain which words mean exactly what they say and which words do not.

Final Syllables *-tion, -ture*

Circle the word that names the picture.

1. vulture / value / vacation	**2.** $\frac{1}{2}$ fiction / fracture / fraction	**3.** **?** queenly / question / quotation
4. potter / potion / pasture	**5.** noodle / nation / nowhere	**7.** posture / picture / pebble
7. caption / capture / caution	**8.** FUN IN THE SUN lotion / lecture / ladle	**9.** notion / nature / never
10. traction / teacher / texture	**11.** section / scary / sculpture	**12.** station / stature / stampede

Read It Together   The structure near the pasture is a bus station.

Name _____ Date _____

Story Time

Write a word from the box to complete each sentence.

High Frequency **Words**
example
got
music
sing
song
state
still
story
tell
today

1. Morgan goes to summer camp in the

_____ of New York.

2. Every Sunday night is music night. The campers sit in a

circle and _____ camp songs.

3. Every Friday night is story night. A camper can _____ any kind of story.

4. For _____, Morgan told a spooky story last Friday night.

5. Some campers _____ scared when Morgan told her story.

6. They _____ jump when they hear loud noises!

7. It is Friday _____. What story would you tell the other campers?

Grammar: Prepositions

Use Prepositions

Directions:

1. Make a spinner.

2. Play with a partner.

3. Take turns spinning the spinner.

4. Read the word. Say a sentence using the preposition you land on. Then have your partner say whether the preposition in your sentence shows time or direction.

Make a Spinner

1. Put a paper clip ▭ in the center of the circle.

2. Hold one end of the paper clip with a pencil.

3. Spin the paper clip around the pencil.

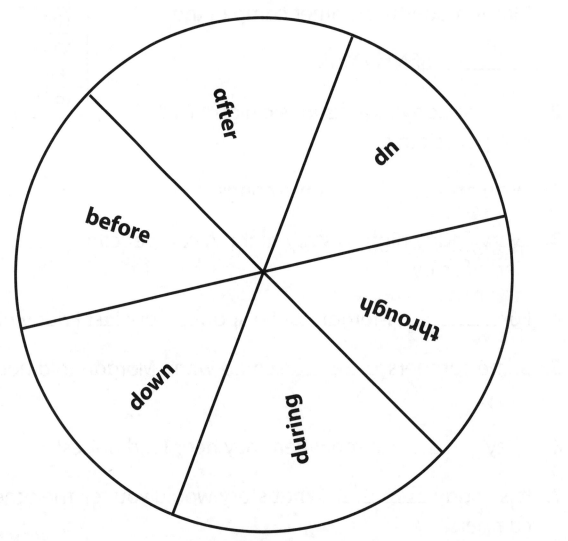

Phonics

Final Syllables *-tion, -ture*

Write the word that completes each sentence.

1. education   moisture   lotion

The children at Pine Street School get a great _____.

2. nation   instruction   capture

Teachers give them _____ in a lot of subjects.

3. section   caption   addition

In math class, they learn _____ and subtraction.

4. mixture   fiction   furniture

In English class, they read books that are _____.

5. pictures   lectures   portions

In art class, they paint different kinds of _____.

6. question   mention   nature

The students go outside to study _____.

7. attention   futures   creatures

They see many living _____.

8. fraction   vulture   donation

Once they saw a _____ circling in the sky.

9. cultures   stations   features

They learned that a bald head is one of its _____.

Name _____ Date _____

Final Syllables -*sion*, -*cian*

Write the words to complete each sentence.

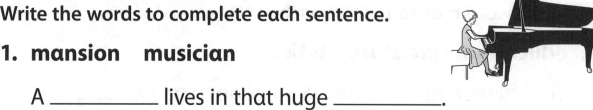

1. mansion   musician

A _____ lives in that huge _____.

2. electrician   television

She calls an _____ to help her with the wires for her new _____.

3. permission   magician

Then she gives her friend the _____ her _____ to perform a show.

4. decision   admission

The friends make a _____ to give children free _____ to the show.

5. division   sessions

So many children come that there is a _____ of the show into two _____.

6. expression   musician

In one, the _____ plays music with _____.

7. magician   vision

In the other, the _____ plays tricks on the children's _____.

Grammar and Writing

Write Prepositions

Read the story. Then write the word from the box that correctly completes each sentence.

across	before	through	after	to	down

Welcome to our special celebration of America.

Did you walk __*to*__ the park or ride in a car? You

can walk to many exhibits _____ the hill. You can

get your lunch ticket in the big tent. Be sure to go

there _____ lunch. To find the international café,

walk _____ the bridge. _____ lunch, you can

see the exhibits. To get to the exhibits, go _____

the gates.

Grammar: Prepositions

Use Prepositions

Grammar Rules Prepositions

Some prepositions show location.	→	in, on, above, over, below, under, beside, next to
Some prepositions show direction.	→	up, down, through, across, into, around

Circle the word to complete each sentence. Then read the sentence.

1. The pot is <u>under/on</u> the stove.

2. Dad puts noodles <u>into/across</u> the pot.

3. I stand <u>next to/above</u> Dad.

4. I stir the noodles <u>around/down</u> with a spoon.

5. The flag is <u>beside/through</u> the stove.

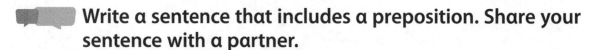 **Write a sentence that includes a preposition. Share your sentence with a partner.**

Phonics

Words with Schwa

Circle the word that names the picture.

1. garden	2.	3.
gerbil gallon (garden)	person pardon pencil	puffin parcel pretzel
4.	**5.**	**6.**
ribbon royal reason	shovel station shorten	wiggle wagon waken
7.	**8.**	**9.**
apple apron action	squirrel shorten squirted	satin slogan signal
10.	**11.**	**12.**
jacket jackal juggle	channel chisel chicken	seven sandal season

 **Read It Together**   Do you wear an apron, a sandal, or a ribbon on your foot?

Name _____ Date _____

Author's Purpose

Make an author's purpose chart to tell about a nonfiction text you have read.

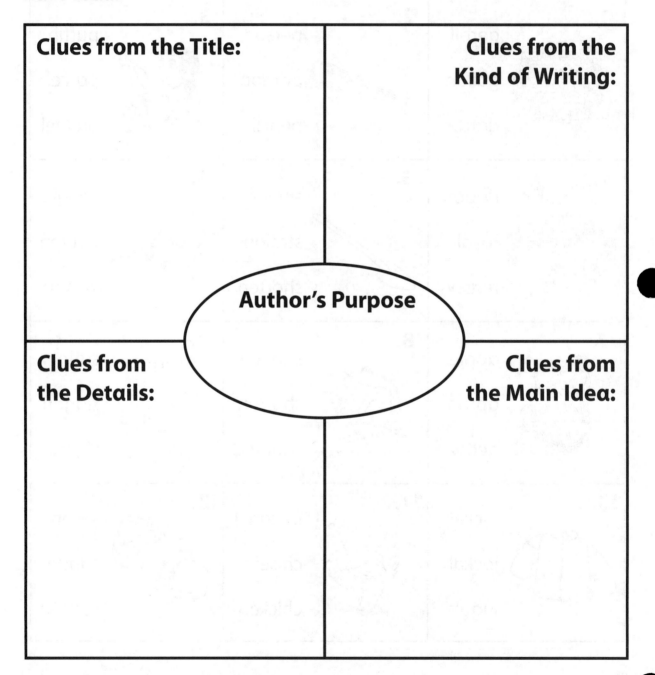

Clues from the Title:

Clues from the Kind of Writing:

Author's Purpose

Clues from the Details:

Clues from the Main Idea:

 Share your chart with a partner and compare authors' purposes.

Name _____ Date _____

Words with Schwa

Write the words to complete each sentence.

1. person   medal

My grandma is a _____ who should get a _____.
She does everything!

2. kitchen   apron

Sometimes she puts on her _____ and makes goodies

in the _____.

3. muffins   lemon

She is a baker. She bakes the best _____ _____!

4. mitten   woolen

She is a knitter. She knits warm _____ things. Each hat

and _____ is perfect!

5. musical   vocal

She is a _____ star in _____ shows in the city.

6. wooden   model

Grandma is a _____ maker. We make _____
airplanes together.

7. petal   garden

When she works in her _____, Grandma is like a farmer.

She knows every _____ and leaf on her plants.

● Word Cards: Words with Schwa

sailor	flower	pencil	capital
kitchen	player	mother	gallon
flavor	cotton	fallen	Megan
nickel	payer	father	signal
listen	Mexican	council	button
kicker	cellar	teacher	American
chicken	carol	evil	pretzel

●High Frequency Word Cards

ride	big
close	home
sleep	new
cry	bed
● show	floor
green	life
plant	came
hurt	sure
jump	left
● please	ate

For use with TE p. T503i   **PM8.28**   Unit 8 | Our United States

Name _____ Date _____

Final Syllables -ent, -ant

Circle the word that names the picture.

1. (student) stable stubble	**2.** pencil panther parent	**3.** infant instant insist
4. toaster talent target	**5.** doormat distant duster	**7.** music magnet merchant
7. protect present pretest	**8.** serpent servant settle	**9.** actor agent absent
10. cellar constant cement	**11.** exit event eagle	**12.** sunset silent seven

Read It Together Are the absent students distant or in class?

For use with TE p. T509c   **PM8.29**   **Unit 8** | Our United States

Name _____   Date _____

A Bed for Carla's Puppy

Write a word from the box to complete each sentence.

High Frequency **Words**
ate
bed
big
came
floor
home
left
life
new
sure

Carla got a brand _____ bed for her

puppy to sleep in. She put the big bed on the _____

in her bedroom. On Tuesday morning when Carla

_____ for school, the puppy was asleep in the bed.

Then the puppy got hungry and _____ some of the

bed. When Carla _____ back home, there was a big

hole in the bed. Carla looked at her puppy and said,

"You _____ are cute, but with you around, _____

will never be boring!"

● Word Cards: Prepositional Phrases

across	down	off	over
through	to	toward	up
bus	desert	city	skyscraper
car	barn	road	mountain
street	log	flag	stairs
swamp	creek	gate	valley
forest	waterfall	beach	hill

For use with TE p. T503l   **PM8.31**   **Unit 8** | Our United States

Name _____ Date _____

Final Syllables *-ent, -ant*

Write the words to complete each sentence.

1. president   important

I am _____ because I am the leader of a country.

I am a _____.

2. innocent   infant

I am small and _____, and I need a lot of care.

I am an _____.

3. absent   student

On most days I am in school, but sometimes I am

_____. I am a _____.

4. parent   constant

I have children who need _____ attention.

I am a _____.

5. elephant   different

I am an animal that is _____ because I have a

trunk. I am an _____.

6. vacant   occupant

This house is not _____ because I live in it.

I am the _____.

Grammar and Writing

Write Prepositional Phrases

Read the story. Then choose the prepositional phrase from the box that correctly completes each sentence. Write the phrase.

on their shirts	in February	of March
on Valentine's Day	to our friends	during the year

There are many fun holidays _____ *during the year* _____.

One of them is Valentine's Day. This holiday

is _____. That is the day we give

special cards _____. Everything is red

_____. That changes just a month later

on the 17th _____. That is when we

celebrate St. Patrick's Day. People wear green. They

put little plants called shamrocks _____.

Name _____ Date _____

America Is . . .

Make an author's purpose chart. Figure out the author's purpose for writing "America Is . . ."

Clues from the Title:

"America Is . . . "

The selection is about America.

Clues from the Kind of Writing:

Literary nonfiction presents facts and ideas in an interesting way.

Author's Purpose

Clues from the Details:

Clues from the Main Idea:

 Work with a partner. Compare the author's purposes that you found.

Name _____   Date _____

Syllables

Circle the word that names the picture.

1. pencil / (puzzle) / paper	**2.** ruler / rubber / raisin	**3.** caption / cabin / capture
4. aside / ajar / asleep	**5.** action / arrive / airplane	**6.** baseball / bobcat / beanbag
7. razor / raindrop / raccoon	**8.** question / quotation / quickly	**9.** stubborn / student / starfish
10. velvet / vulture / vacation	**11.** address / adore / adult	**12.** creatures / crackles / craters

Read It Together   Some creatures are asleep near the cabin.

For use with TE p. T527o   **PM8.35**   **Unit 8 | Our United States**

Name _____ Date _____

Syllables

Write the words to complete each sentence.

1. thousands   jungle

There are _____ of plants and animals living in a rain

forest _____.

2. important   reason

That's one _____ that these forests are _____.

3. plants   illness

We use some of the _____ to fight _____.

4. location   equator

The _____ of some rain forests is near the _____.

5. treetops   around

It is sunny and windy _____ the tallest _____.

6. reptiles   leafy

Many _____, mammals, and insects live in the

_____ parts of the trees.

7. floor   biggest

The _____ animals live in the darkest part, on the

forest _____.

● Word Cards: Multisyllabic Words

tree	musician	skyscraper	circle
happiness	important	landform	explain
color	along	fly	white
fact	upbringing	duty	continent
vacation	united	bemuse	freedom
test	faithful	understand	same
compare	lot	travel	reunion

● High Frequency Word Cards

will	man
soon	best
black	lot
brown	face
● group	same
high	fly
leave	tree
study	color
open	white
● point	bring

Name _____ Date _____

Compare Author's Purpose

Make a comparison chart. Show how "America Is . . ." and "This Land Is Your Land" are the same and how they are different.

	"America Is . . ." by Louise Borden	"This Land Is Your Land" by Woody Guthrie
persuade readers		✓
inform readers	✓	
entertain readers		
share experiences		
express feelings		
express creativity		

 Share your chart with a partner. Take turns comparing the authors' purposes in each selection.

Syllable Division

Divide the syllables and then circle the word that names the picture.

1. extra eager (eagle)	**2.** cactus capture cable

3. donut
dolphin
doghouse

4. photo
oval
open

5. menu
medal
major

7. tunnel
turtle
table

7. cancel
camel
candle

8. stable
stumble
staple

9. sailfish
saddle
sandwich

10. poodle
puddle
pebble

11. needle
napkin
nonstop

12. lumber
little
lobster

Read It Together Do eagles, giraffes, or lobsters fly in the sky?

Name _____ Date _____

An Airplane Trip

Write a word from the box to complete each sentence.

High Frequency **Words**
best
bring
color
face
fly
lot
man
same
tree
white

1. Do you go on airplane trips a _____?

2. I don't, but I will _____ on a plane today.

3. I will _____ my suitcase with me.

4. It is _____ but has splotches of a bright red color.

5. It is the _____ suitcase because it is easy to find!

6. A man with a big grin on his _____ will be waiting for me when I get off the plane!

7. When I get to Grandpa's house, I will climb the _____ to the same fort we made when I was little!

Grammar: Prepositional Phrases

Use Prepositional Phrases

Directions:

1. Make a spinner.

2. Play with a partner.

3. First say a short sentence about America. Then spin the spinner and read the word.

4. Have your partner say your sentence with a prepositional phrase that adds more details. He or she must use the preposition you land on. Then switch roles.

Make a Spinner

1. Put a paper clip ⌐⊐ in the center of the circle.

2. Hold one end of the paper clip with a pencil.

3. Spin the paper clip around the pencil.

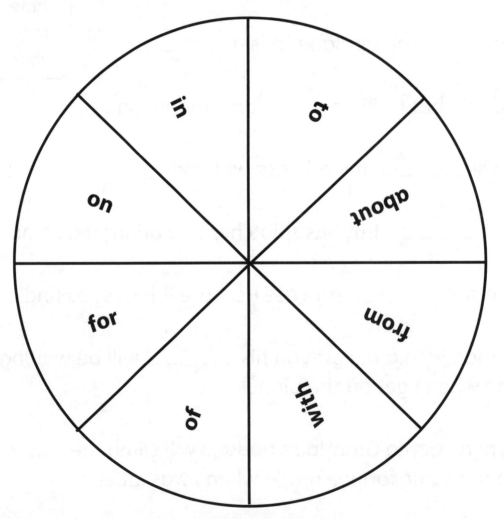

Name _____ Date _____

Syllable Division

Divide the syllables. Then write the word that completes each sentence.

1. **number   dolphin   nature**

   A _____ swims in the sea, but it is a mammal.

2. **hundreds   candles   robins**

   Sometimes _____ of these graceful animals swim together in a big group.

3. **tiptoe   open   turtle**

   A loggerhead sea _____ swims in the sea, too.

4. **simple   reptile   kitchen**

   It is a _____ , not a mammal.

5. **explains   adults   flippers**

   It uses its _____ to glide and steer through the water.

6. **also   circle   recall**

   Sharks _____ swim in the sea, but they are fish.

7. **sparkle   around   nation**

   Sharks have been _____ for a very, very long time!

8. **Locate   Visit   Pretend**

   _____ you are swimming in the sea. What other animals might you see?

Grammar and Writing

Write Prepositional Phrases

Read the story. Then choose the words from the box that correctly complete each sentence.

of interesting people and places	out the door
for the National Geographic Society	during the year
about his photograph	around America

Sam Abell travels _____ around America _____

taking pictures. He may visit many different states

_____. His pictures

include many different subjects. They are photos

_____. He provides photos

_____. Here is what Sam

Abell says _____: "It's what

gets me _____."

Grammar: Prepositional Phrases

Use Prepositional Phrases

1. **Partner 1 points to a sentence.**

2. **Partner 2 points to a prepositional phrase.**

3. **If the cards make a clear sentence, color in the squares. If not, begin again.**

4. **Play until all the squares are colored.**

Sentences

Sentence Starters

We go _____ .	Teresa and I write _____ .	Koji and Lynn have fun _____ .	You and I read _____ .

Prepositional Phrases

to the park	after breakfast	during the concert	into the monument
along the coast	with the map	about American history	under the blue sky